OBJECT-ORIENTED PHP

OBJECT-ORIENTED PHP

Concepts, Techniques, and Code

by Peter Lavin

**NO STARCH
PRESS**

San Francisco

Publisher: William Pollock
Managing Editor: Elizabeth Campbell
Associate Production Editor: Christina Samuell
Cover and Interior Design: Octopod Studios
Developmental Editor: William Pollock
Technical Reviewer: Peter MacIntyre
Copyeditors: Publication Services, Inc. and Sarah Lemaire
Compositor: Riley Hoffman
Proofreader: Stephanie Provines

For information on book distributors or translations, please contact No Starch Press, Inc. directly:

No Starch Press, Inc.
555 De Haro Street, Suite 250, San Francisco, CA 94107
phone: 415.863.9900; fax: 415.863.9950; info@nostarch.com; www.nostarch.com

Library of Congress Cataloging-in-Publication Data

```
Lavin, Peter.
 Object-oriented PHP : concepts, techniques, and code / Peter Lavin.
     p. cm.
 Includes index.
 ISBN 1-59327-077-1
1. PHP (Computer program language) 2.  Object-oriented programming (Computer science)  I. Title.
QA76.73.P224L38 2006
 005.1'17--dc22
                                      2006015309
```

BRIEF CONTENTS

CONTENTS IN DETAIL

4
SHOW A LITTLE CLASS   17

5
MOD UR CLASS   25

6
THE THUMBNAILIMAGE CLASS   35

10
IMPROVEMENT THROUGH INHERITANCE 75

11
ADVANCED OBJECT-ORIENTED PROGRAMMING
CONCEPTS 91

12
KEEPING IT FRESH 99

13
MORE MAGIC METHODS

14
CREATING DOCUMENTATION USING
THE REFLECTION CLASSES

15
EXTENDING SQLITE

16
USING PDO

A
SETTING UP PHP 5

B
CONVERSION TABLE: PHP 4 AND PHP 5

GLOSSARY

INDEX

ACKNOWLEDGMENTS

Special thanks to my family for their support, encouragement, and forbearance; to the folks at No Starch for so deftly smoothing over the rough edges; and lastly, thanks to Rasmus Lerdorf, creator of PHP.

INTRODUCTION

A number of years ago, before I started using PHP, I created dynamic web pages using C. This really wasn't too different from some of the other options available at the time, though it seems almost unthinkable now. Creating a dynamic page meant outputting HTML from your script and recompiling that script if any changes needed to be made. What PHP had to offer was the ability to embed server-side scripts into the body of a page wherever they were needed. This was a considerable improvement because it meant you could code the HTML as HTML and insert scripting when required. Introducing changes was much easier, and since PHP is an interpreted language, there was no need for recompilation.

The paths to using PHP are many and varied, but the single most important reason for staying with it is ease of use. This is the major reason that PHP has become such a popular web programming language. With the arrival of version 5, PHP once again makes life simpler for web developers. You can now add the power of a robust but uncomplicated object-oriented (OO) language to your arsenal of web development tools.

What Does This Book Have to Offer?

This book teaches OO PHP by doing it. If you are a PHP programmer who wants to make the switch to an OO approach, *Object-Oriented PHP* can ease the transition from procedural to object-oriented programming (OOP). Basic concepts are introduced using simple but useful classes. In short, this book:

- Brings together information from a variety of sources for a comprehensive overview of OO PHP
- Explains OO concepts through concrete examples, not in the abstract
- Takes a practical and easy-to-understand approach
- Demonstrates the advantages of OOP rather than just asserting them

The classes developed in this book are fully functional and are all available for download at the companion website. This code can be put to work immediately in a variety of situations.

The code takes full advantage of the capabilities of PHP 5 but, where possible, a PHP 4 version of the code is also provided, because you don't always have a choice about where your code is deployed. Additionally, this will ease the transition for anyone already familiar with OOP under PHP 4.

Who Should Read This Book?

This book will appeal to the developer who is familiar with PHP and wants to learn how to use its OO capabilities. However, programmers already familiar with an OO language, such as Java, who want to learn a scripting language will also find it useful. Additionally, if you are a system administrator who is considering installing PHP 5, this book will help you make an informed decision.

PHP is first and foremost a language for creating dynamic web pages, but the relative simplicity of OOP in PHP makes it an ideal language for a general introduction to OOP. The concepts learned here are applicable to any OO language, so if you want to get a feel for OOP, OO PHP is a good place to begin.

Whatever your motivation, by the time you've finished this book you'll have an excellent understanding of OOP and numerous classes that can easily be reused in a variety of circumstances. But, more importantly, you'll be able to create your own classes and extend existing ones.

Requirements

In order to get the maximum benefit from this book, there are software and skill prerequisites.

Software

With one or two minor exceptions (they are noted in the text), all the code in this book will run on PHP 5.0.4 and higher. The PHP 4 code will run just fine under PHP 5 but will issue warnings if error reporting is set to E_STRICT. (See Appendix A for more information about this new error reporting level.)

PHP is available for virtually any operating system, so there are no restrictions in this regard. As far as databases are concerned, any recent version of MySQL, specifically versions 3 or higher, will do. Apache is the preferred web server but Internet Information Server (IIS) can also be used. (However, the acronym for Windows using IIS and MySQL with PHP may serve to dissuade you from using this particular platform.)

Skills

Some knowledge of PHP is desirable, but barring that, a good understanding of C-type syntax should get you through most code examples. Some knowledge of (X)HTML and CSS is also assumed—after all, PHP is primarily a web development language. You need only the most basic understanding of XML even when working with the `SimpleXMLElement` or `SOAPClient` classes. Some understanding of JavaScript would be beneficial.

Familiarity with relational databases, especially MySQL, is recommended.

Overview of Contents

OOP is often described as an iterative process, and this is the approach we take in this book. We will develop working examples of classes in order to explore specific OO concepts and then return to improve these classes.

This book has sixteen chapters and two appendices. It is made up of three different sections. The first three chapters offer an introduction to OOP as implemented in PHP. Chapters 4 through 9 develop some useful classes that demonstrate the basic syntax and concepts of OOP. Code compatible with PHP 4 and PHP 5 is provided. The remainder of the book makes use of built-in classes available in PHP 5 only; consequently, there is no PHP 4–compatible code. A brief outline of each chapter is provided here.

Chapter 1

Strangely enough, there are still web developers who question whether a scripting language really needs to be object-oriented. This chapter deals with issues related to this question.

Chapter 2

This chapter introduces the basics of OOP. The intent is not to exhaustively cover the theoretical underpinnings of OOP—far from it. Think of this chapter as a quick check for shallow water and rocks before diving in. The concepts discussed are class, access modifiers, and inheritance—all you need to start coding as quickly as possible.

Chapter 3

This chapter gives a broad overview of the changes introduced with PHP 5. If you are new to PHP, it's a good opportunity to assess the capabilities of the language, but it should also appeal to the PHP 4 programmer who's considering upgrading. This chapter also deals with some compatibility issues when moving from version 4 to version 5.

Chapter 4

Hands-on programming begins here. A relatively straightforward class is coded in the style of PHP 4. The most basic concept of OOP, a class, is introduced.

Chapter 5

The directory items class, created in Chapter 4, is upgraded to use the syntax of PHP 5. Further functionality is added to this class.

Chapter 6

This chapter creates a thumbnail image class for reducing images on the fly. This class is used in conjunction with the directory items class created in Chapter 5 to display images of a uniform size.

Chapter 7

After dealing with the size of images, the problem of displaying a large number of images is addressed. A page navigator class is created in order to step through numerous images in an orderly fashion.

Chapter 8

Creating one class has lead to the creation of two other classes. This chapter demonstrates that these classes can work well in unison.

Chapter 9

Databases are an important element in most dynamic web pages. Creating our own MySQL database classes highlights the advantages of OOP in this area. Using the page navigator class in a different context demonstrates the reusability of OO code.

Chapter 10

Inheritance can improve the performance and ease of use of the MySQL database classes. Catching exceptions is cleaner and much less tedious than error trapping.

Chapter 11

In the interest of getting on with the coding, some advanced concepts of OOP were glossed over in Chapter 10. This chapter returns to some of the topics previously raised. It includes an in-depth discussion of abstract classes, interfaces, and static classes. Design patterns and polymorphism are also examined.

Chapter 12

PHP is all about creating dynamic websites. So far we've seen how this can be done using databases. This chapter explores the creation of dynamic pages using the SimpleXMLElement and SOAPClient classes. This chapter also shows how asynchronous JavaScript and XML (AJAX) can work in unison with PHP. See just how easy it is to implement web services using classes built in to PHP 5.

Chapter 13

This is one of the few non–project-oriented chapters. It explores in detail all the magic methods available in PHP 5. Understanding these methods is essential for getting the maximum benefit out of OO PHP and for avoiding some common "gotchas."

Chapter 14

PHP 5 includes a group of classes called the Reflection classes, typically used to reverse engineer code. Pay a little attention to the format of internal documentation, and these classes can be used to make your code self-documenting.

Chapter 15

SQLite is packaged with PHP 5 and comes with an OO interface. This chapter extends SQLite and develops a web-based resource management program. No knowledge of SQLite is presupposed.

Chapter 16

PHP Data Object (PDO) is a data-access abstraction layer that works with most databases. The application developed in Chapter 15 is converted to a PDO application.

Appendix A

This appendix deals with OO issues related to the installation and configuration of PHP 5.

Appendix B

The major syntactic differences between PHP 4 and PHP 5 are presented here in tabular form.

Companion Website

This book has a companion website (http://objectorientedphp.com) where you can download all the code related to it. Downloads are available as zipped files or tarballs, chapter by chapter or as one complete download. Code compatible with PHP 4 is clearly marked as such and, depending upon your circumstances, may not need to be downloaded at all.

The principle purpose of the companion site is to provide these downloads, but working examples of some of the classes created in this book are also incorporated into the site. The DirectoryItems class is used to present the downloads, and a page navigator is used in conjunction with MySQL classes to page through a database of articles. Resources are added and displayed using PDO and an SQLite database. Finally, documentation of internal PHP classes is generated using the Documenter class. The companion website not only provides support for this book, it is also a graphic demonstration of its contents; to rephrase an expression, "the message becomes the medium."

You can also post or review errata on the website, and links to many of the resources used in this book are provided.

Resources

For your convenience, some of the most useful resources are reproduced here.

Websites

International PHP Magazine: www.phpmag.net
Cutting-edge articles and news about PHP. Available by subscription only.

PHP.net: http://php.net
The official PHP site, where you will find documentation and many code examples. It is the primary source of information about PHP.

php|architect: http://phparchitect.com
A monthly magazine for PHP professionals. Available by subscription only.

Planet PHP: www.planet-php.net
Links to articles and all the latest news about PHP.

Zend: www.zend.com
Information about Zend products, but also many good tutorials by the creators of the scripting engine that underlies PHP.

Books

Essential PHP Security, by Chris Shiflett (O'Reilly)

Learning XML, by Erik T. Ray (O'Reilly)

PHP 5 Power Programming, by Andi Gutmans, Stig Bakken, and Derick Rethans (Prentice Hall)

PHP Cookbook, by David Sklar and Adam Trachtenberg (O'Reilly)

PHP Hacks, by Jack D. Herrington (O'Reilly)

php|architect's Guide to PHP Design Patterns, by Jason Sweat (php|architect)

php|architect's Guide to PHP Security, by Ilia Alshanetsky (php|architect)

Programming PHP, by Kevin Tatroe, Peter MacIntyre, and Rasmus Lerdorf (O'Reilly)

Thinking in Java, by Bruce Eckel (Prentice Hall)

Upgrading to PHP 5, by Adam Trachtenberg (O'Reilly)

1

WHAT A TANGLED WEB WE WEAVE

Creating a web page ain't what it used to be. Setting up a website today usually means incorporating numerous technologies, among them (X)HTML, CSS, JavaScript, SQL, and a server-side scripting language. But that's not all—a web page also runs within a browser. There are several different browsers, of course, and each behaves differently. Not only that, but different versions of the same browser can act differently, and even the same version of the same browser can't be relied upon to behave the same when running on different operating systems, with different hardware, different screen resolutions, and so on.

Add to this the various configuration files—for the scripting language and the web server, for example—which also affect the display of a particular web page, and you can see that the web developer's lot is not a happy one.

It may not be readily apparent that an object-oriented (OO) approach is a means of simplifying this situation. OO development might be seen as symptomatic of the larger problem. To the embattled web developer an OO approach can appear to be just another complication of what's already a messy business.

Do We Really Need Objects?

The ability of any server-side scripting language to "include" files within a web page reduces initial work and ongoing maintenance. For instance, suppose a website contains a menu at the top of each web page, and this menu is identical throughout the site. You could cut and paste the appropriate code into every page, but this is both cumbersome and counterproductive. It's much better to write the code once and use a server-side scripting language to insert the menu wherever it's needed. That way, should an update be required, you can make one change to one file rather than changing many files. This makes site-wide updates much easier.

You could summarize this approach as "include and reuse; don't rewrite." In a sense, object-oriented programming (OOP) is just an extension of this concept. Objects simplify web development by eliminating the need to cut, paste, and adapt existing code. If the usefulness of OOP were this evident, it would meet with little resistance. This has not been the case, however. Let's look at some of the more interesting objections to OO web development to remove any nagging doubts you may have.

Just a Scripting Language

PHP is a scripting language. Some of the objections to OOP focus on this fact.

Some scripting languages simply string together a series of commands and for this reason are sometimes referred to as "glue."[1] A shell script, for example, may combine a number of operating system commands in order to eliminate the tedium of repetitively typing the same thing. The variety of requirements of a web page might seem to support the view that PHP is just this sort of scripting language—it provides a glue to hold together the disparate elements of a web page. If this is all that PHP does, then there is probably no need for it to be object-oriented. In fact, object orientation might even be a disadvantage. In this view, which is sometimes expressed with a degree of condescension, OO capabilities are best left to full-blown programming languages and are an unnecessary encumbrance for a scripting language. An OO scripting language is a contradiction in terms; it's a language that's "getting above itself."[2]

To some extent, the limited OO capabilities of PHP 4 reinforced the view that a scripting language shouldn't attempt to be object-oriented. PHP 4 looked like a half-hearted attempt to jump on the OO bandwagon. Because it was missing some of the major elements associated with OOP, it was easy to dismiss OO PHP as a wannabe OO language. It simply lacked the tools of a serious OO language. In light of the much-improved OO capabilities of PHP 5, this view needs to be reassessed.

---

[1] You'll even find this description on the PHP site (http://php.net). In the FAQ on installation, PHP is described as "the glue used to build cool web applications."

[2] For a recent variation on this argument see "James Gosling: Java Is Under No Serious Threat from PHP, Ruby C#," available at www.sys-con.tv/read/193146.htm. There, James Gosling argues that "they are scripting languages and get their power through specialization: they just generate web pages." (Accessed March 19, 2006.)

Chapter 3 deals with the improvements to PHP's object model in version 5. With these improvements, PHP is now a full-blown OO language. It should be judged by how well it does the job, not on the basis of a preconceived notion of what a scripting language should or shouldn't do. After all, a programming language, scripting or otherwise, is just a tool, a means to an end. Tools are meant to be judged not by what they are, but by what they can do.

Object Orientation Is for Large Software Shops

Another argument against OOP goes like this: OOP is something best left to the large shops. If a number of programmers are involved in the same project, an OO approach is a necessary evil, but it's not much use for the lone developer. Because big software shops have many different programmers doing somewhat specialized jobs, the modular, OO approach is required. It is not something that the lone developer needs to worry about. The lone developer doesn't have to coordinate his efforts with others, so a procedural approach is the better way.

This point of view correctly identifies the fact that an OO approach is more modular and thus more suitable to an environment that requires collaboration. It is also true that in some circumstances a single developer can do a superior job—too many cooks *can* spoil the broth. And it is probably also true that taking an OO approach will slow development. But an OO solution takes more time than a procedural one *only the first time that the solution is created*. The lone developer can benefit from the reusability and adaptability of an OO solution just like any large software shop can.

Leave Well Enough Alone

We've dealt with some of the reasoned arguments against an OO approach to web development, but in many cases what's at work is simply a reluctance to change. PHP has been exceptionally successful as a procedural language. If it ain't broke, why fix it?

Computer languages, like their natural counterparts, must keep pace with changes in the environment or risk becoming irrelevant. OOP doesn't replace procedural programming or make it obsolete. Nor is an OO approach always the right approach, as some OO enthusiasts might have you believe. However, some web problems require an OO solution. Additionally, without a minimal understanding of the basics of OOP, you can't make full use of the capabilities of PHP 5. For instance, if you want to create a SOAP client, there is really no other way to do it than by using the SOAPClient class.

There's no requirement that once you start programming using an OO approach you need always code this way. PHP is a hybrid language with OO capabilities grafted onto it. You can use an OO approach when you want and otherwise revert to procedural programming.

Increased Complexity

Fear of PHP becoming overly complex is often a more subtly stated objection to an OO PHP. There's no doubt that OOP can sometimes introduce unwanted complexity—just look at multiple inheritance in C++ or Enterprise Java, for example. This hasn't happened with PHP, and there's good reason to suspect that it won't. PHP is first and foremost a web development language (which is probably why it has taken so long for PHP to adopt an OO approach). Web programming is a specialized form of programming, and OO capabilities have been introduced to serve this end. The fact that PHP's implementation of OOP doesn't always make OO purists happy is indicative of this. Even as a procedural language, PHP was never about being pretty or being a model language; it has always been about solving web problems.

A quick look at the culture of PHP should convince you that PHP is unlikely to develop into an overly complex language.

The PHP Culture

Culture is not something that is usually associated with a programming language, but looking at the culture of PHP will help you understand PHP's implementation of OOP. PHP is an open-source language created more than 10 years ago by Rasmus Lerdorf. It has all the hallmarks of a successful open-source project: It has been around for a number of years, it is continually being upgraded, it has a robust developer community, and it has continuity of leadership—Rasmus Lerdorf still takes a very active role in its development.

PHP is by far the most popular web development language, and the major reason for its success is ease of use. This is no accident. It is easy to use because it was conceived as a language to simplify web development.[3] This has not been forgotten with PHP's upgrade to a full-blown OO language. For example, one of the new classes introduced in PHP 5 is the aptly named SimpleXMLElement. With this class you can incorporate an RSS feed into a web page using only four lines of code (see Chapter 12).

The point of object orientation in PHP is not to turn PHP into Java or something similar, but to provide the proper tools for web developers. Object orientation is another strategy for adapting to the current circumstances of web development.

NOTE   *The impetus to "Keep It Simple, Stupid" is alive and well (and, as it happens, living in Paris). At a recent meeting of PHP core developers, the introduction of a new keyword was rejected as "against the KISS approach of PHP" (minutes, PHP Developers Meeting, Paris, November 11 and 12, 2005).*

Unquestionably, there will be a learning curve for a procedural programmer adopting an OO approach to web development, but you'll quickly pick up on PHP's implementation of OOP. In fact, you'll probably find that some of the tasks you're used to doing procedurally are more easily done in an OO manner. I suspect that once you've started on the OO path, you'll find more and more uses for it.

---

[3] See Rasmus Lerdorf, "Do You PHP?" available at www.oracle.com/technology/pub/articles/php_experts/rasmus_php.html. (Accessed March 14, 2006.)

2

BASICS OF OBJECT-ORIENTED PROGRAMMING

This chapter is aimed at an audience unfamiliar with the basic concepts of object-oriented programming (OOP). The intent is to provide a general overview of OOP with a view toward using PHP effectively. We'll restrict the discussion to a few basic concepts of OOP as it relates to PHP, though it is sometimes useful to look at other object-oriented (OO) languages such as Java or C++.

We'll discuss three aspects of object orientation in this chapter: class, access modifiers, and inheritance. Although OOP may be a different programming paradigm, in many respects it's an extension of procedural programming, so where appropriate, I'll use examples from procedural programming to help explain these concepts. Later chapters will return to the topics introduced here and refine them through the use of concrete examples.

Class

You can't have OOP without objects, and that's what classes provide. At the simplest level, a *class* is a data type. However, unlike primitive data types such as an integer, a float, or a character, a class is a complex, user-defined data type. A class is similar to a database record in that it encapsulates the characteristics of an object. For example, the record of a Person might contain a birth date, an address, a name, and a phone number. A class is a data type made up of other data types that together describe an object.

Classes Versus Records

Although a class is like a record, an important difference is that classes contain functions as well as different data types. And, when a function becomes part of a data type, procedural programming is turned on its head, quite literally, as you can see in the following example syntax. A function call that looked like this:

```
function_call($somevariable);
```

looks something like this with OOP:

```
$somevariable->function_call();
```

The significant difference here is that OO variables don't have things done to them; they do things. They are the actors rather than the acted upon, and for this reason they are said to behave. The *behavior* of a class is the sum of its functions.

A Cohesive Whole

Procedural programmers often work with code libraries. These libraries usually group related functions together. For instance, all database functions might be grouped together in a file called dbfunctions.inc. The functions that make up an object's behavior should also be related to one another, but in a much stronger fashion than functions in the same library. Just as the different elements of a Person record describe an individual, so too should the behavior of a class describe the class. In order for something to be an object, it should be a cohesive whole incorporating appropriate characteristics and appropriate behavior.

Objects Are Instances

Classes aren't themselves objects, but a way of creating objects—they are templates or blueprints that form the model for an object. When speaking loosely, these two terms are sometimes used interchangeably, but strictly speaking an *object* is an instance of a class. This is somewhat like the difference between the concept of an integer and a specific variable $x with a specific value. The concept of a class as a template for an object becomes clearer in the context of inheritance, especially when we discuss multiple inheritance (a topic we'll deal with shortly).

Objects Need Access Modifiers

OOP is made possible by using this simple concept of a class as a cohesive aggregate of characteristics and behaviors—as you'll see in Chapter 3, this is exactly what objects are in PHP 4—but one of the most important features of any OO language is the use of access modifiers. *Access modifiers* refine the object model by controlling how an object is used or reused. Simply put, access modifiers provide guidance about what you can and cannot do with an object. To get a sense of what this means, let's use an example from procedural programming.

Let's define a *subroutine* as a function that is never invoked directly but that is only called by other functions. Now suppose you're a procedural programmer with a library of functions and subroutines that is used by several other programmers. The ability to flag subroutines as secondary would be helpful in instructing others how to use your library, but the only way to do this is through documentation. However, in OOP, access modifiers not only indicate the primacy of certain functions over others, they enforce it programmatically. They implement language constraints to ensure that "subroutines" are never called directly. Properly constructed classes are self-documenting and self-regulating.

In the situation just described, the need to document a code library arises because it's used in a collaborative environment; the exact same circumstance accounts for the existence of access modifiers. One of the assumptions of OOP is that it is conducted within an interactive context with access modifiers defining the ways of interacting. This is one of the important differences between OOP and procedural programming. Access modifiers provide the rules for using a class and this syntactically defined "etiquette" is commonly referred to as an *interface*. By providing an interface, there is less need to rely on documentation and on user programmers "doing the right thing."

Documenting code libraries is important because libraries get reused; access modifiers matter for exactly the same reason—they facilitate reuse.

Object Reuse and Inheritance

In a biological sense, a child inherits genes from its parents, and this genetic material conditions the appearance and behavior of the child. In OOP the meaning of *inheritance* is analogous—it is the ability to pass along characteristics and behavior. At first this feature of OOP may seem somehow magical, but really inheritance is just a technique for reusing code—much the way you might include a library of functions in procedural programming.

If you identify an existing class that exactly suits your needs, you can simply use it and benefit from the predefined behavior. Inheritance comes into play when a class doesn't do quite what you want. This situation is not much different from adding functions to an existing code library. Through inheritance you can take advantage of existing behavior but also graft on any additional capabilities you need. For example, if you know that you want to create a Blue jay class and none exists, you can use an existing Bird class by inheriting from it, then modify it to suit your specific situation.

When one class forms the basis for a new class, as a Bird class might for a Blue jay class, the original class is often referred to as the *base* (or *parent*) *class*. For obvious reasons, a class derived from another class is called a *derived class* or a *child class*.

Multiple Inheritance

In nature, multiple inheritance is the norm, but in the world of OO PHP, an object can have only one parent class. The creators of PHP 5 rejected the idea of multiple inheritance for classes. To see why, let's use the Bird class again to show what multiple inheritance is and how it can lead to problems. If you wanted to create a Whooping crane class, it would make sense to derive this class from the Bird class. Suppose you also have an Endangered species class. Multiple inheritance would allow you to create a Whooping crane class from a combination of these two classes. This would seem to be an excellent idea until you realize that both classes define an eating behavior. Which one should you prefer? Awkward situations like this highlight the disadvantages of multiple inheritance. With single inheritance this kind of situation never arises.

Having Your Cake and Eating It Too

Single inheritance offers a simpler and more straightforward approach, but there are times when you may wish to combine behaviors from different classes. A whooping crane *is* both a bird and endangered. It doesn't make sense to build one of these classes from scratch every time you want this combination. Is there a way of combining different classes and avoiding the problem of overlapping behavior?

PHP solves this problem by introducing the concept of an interface. In this context, *interface* means a class with no data members that is made up only of functions that lack an implementation (function prototypes with no bodies). Any class that inherits from an interface must implement the missing function body. If Endangered species were an interface rather than a class, having more than one eating function wouldn't matter. The method definition in the Bird class would act as the implementation of the interface function. In this way interfaces avoid the problem of defining the same function twice.

NOTE   *Because PHP does not require function prototyping, you may be unfamiliar with this concept. A* function prototype *is the declaration of a function name and parameters prior to its use—the function signature, if you like.*

A class may inherit from only one class, but because interfaces lack an implementation any number of them may be inherited. In true PHP fashion, interfaces contribute to a powerful but flexible programming language. (You'll see how useful interfaces are in Chapter 10, where we add the built-in interface Iterator to a database class.)

Interfaces can be described as *abstract* because they always require an implementation. Because they are abstract, interfaces bear more resemblance to templates than classes do. Unlike classes, they can never be used "as is"; they are only meaningful in the context of inheritance. Because interfaces lack an implementation they can act only as a model for creating a derived class.

Where to Go from Here

We've touched on three topics central to OOP: classes, access modifiers, and inheritance. Classes define objects, access modifiers determine how objects can be used, and inheritance makes it easy to adapt objects for different circumstances. I've emphasized the ways in which procedural programming is like OOP with a view to easing the transition to an OO approach, but I've also shown important differences. A data type like a class, which incorporates functions, is unlike anything encountered in procedural programming. Additionally, OOP provides access modifiers to control how an object may be used. Instead of relying on documentation and a disciplined approach, OOP incorporates constraints into the language.

The next chapter discusses the differences between PHP 4 and PHP 5. This will be particularly useful for people already familiar with the OO capabilities of PHP 4 who want an overview of the improvements.

3

OBJECT-ORIENTED FEATURES NEW TO PHP 5

PHP 3 was released in mid-1998. Some basic object-oriented (OO) capabilities were included, more or less as an afterthought, to "provide new ways of accessing arrays."[1] No significant changes were made to the object model when version 4 was released in mid-2000. The basics of object-oriented programming (OOP) were there—you could create a class and single inheritance was supported.

With the release of PHP 5 in 2004 there was plenty of room for improving PHP's OO capabilities. At this point, Java, the most popular OO language to date, had already been around for almost 10 years. Why did it take PHP so long to become a full-fledged OO language? The short answer is because PHP is principally a web development language and the pressures of web development have only recently pushed it in this direction.

---

[1] See Zeev Suraski, "Object-Oriented Evolution of PHP," available at www.devx.com/webdev/Article/10007/0/page/1. (Accessed March 27, 2006.)

Support for objects has been grafted onto the language—you can choose to use objects or simply revert to procedural programming. That PHP is a hybrid language should be viewed as something positive, not as a disadvantage. There are some situations where you will simply want to insert a snippet of PHP and other situations where you will want to make use of its OO capabilities.

As I have already argued in Chapter 1, in some cases, an OO solution is the only solution. PHP 5 recognizes this fact and incorporates a full-blown object model, consolidating PHP's position as the top server-side scripting language.

Like Chapter 2, this will be a chapter of broad strokes. I'll give a general overview of how the object model has been improved, and then I'll get into the details using concrete examples in later chapters. I'll also address the issue of backward compatibility.

Access Modifiers

Chapter 2 identified access modifiers as an essential element of an OO language. PHP 5 gives us everything we would expect in this area. In previous versions of PHP there was no support for data protection, meaning that all elements of a class were publicly accessible. This lack of access modifiers was probably the biggest disincentive to using objects in PHP 4.

NOTE *A notion closely related to data protection is* information hiding. *Access modifiers make information hiding possible by exposing an interface (as defined in Chapter 2). This is also referred to as* encapsulation *of an object.*

Built-in Classes

Every OOP language comes with some built-in classes, and PHP is no exception. PHP 5 introduces the Standard PHP Library (SPL), which provides a number of ready-made classes and interfaces. As of version 5.1, depending upon how PHP is configured, all in all, there are well over 100 built-in classes and interfaces—a healthy increase from the number available in version 5.0.

Having ready-made objects speeds up development, and native classes written in C offer significant performance advantages. Even if these built-in classes don't do exactly what you want, they can easily be extended to suit your needs.

NOTE *There are far too many classes for us to deal with all of them in this book, and some are still not very well documented. We'll focus on the classes that are especially noteworthy.*

Exceptions

All OOP languages support *exceptions*, which are the OO way of handling errors. In order to use exceptions, we need the keywords try, catch, and throw. A *try block* encloses code that may cause an error. If an error occurs, it is thrown and caught by a *catch block*. The advantage of exceptions over errors is that exceptions can be handled centrally, making for much cleaner code. Exceptions also significantly reduce the amount of error-trapping code you need to write, which offers welcome relief from an uninspiring task. Also, having a built-in exception class makes it very easy to create your own customized exceptions through inheritance. (You'll learn how to make the transition from error trapping to exception handling in the section "Replacing Errors with Exceptions" on page 79.)

Database Classes

Because PHP is all about building dynamic web pages, database support is all-important. PHP 5 introduces the mysqli (MySQL Improved) extension with support for the features of MySQL databases versions 4.1 and higher. You can now use features such as prepared statements with MySQL, and you can do so using the built-in OO interface. In fact, anything you can do procedurally can also be done with this interface.

SQLite is a database engine that is incorporated directly into PHP. It is not a general-purpose database like MySQL, but it is an ideal solution in some situations, in many cases producing faster, leaner, and more versatile applications. Again an entirely OO interface is provided.

PHP versions 5.1 and higher also bundle PHP Data Objects (PDO) with the main PHP distribution. If you need to communicate with several different database back ends, then this package is the ideal solution. PDO's common interface for different database systems is only made possible by the new object model.

Given the importance of databases, we'll deal with them extensively in this book. We'll develop a MySQL database class starting with Chapter 9. In Chapter 15 we'll look at SQLite, and in Chapter 16 we'll discuss PDO.

Web Services

In PHP 5 all Extensible Markup Language (XML) support is provided by the libxml2 XML toolkit (www.xmlsoft.org). The underlying code for the Simple API for XML (SAX) and for the Document Object Model (DOM) has been rewritten, and DOM support has been brought in line with the standard defined by the World Wide Web Consortium.

Unified treatment of XML under libxml2 makes for a more efficient and easily maintained implementation. This is particularly important because support for XML under PHP 4 is weak, and web services present many problems that require an OO approach.

Under PHP 4, creating a SOAP client and reading an RSS feed are challenging programming tasks that require creating your own classes or making use of external classes such as NuSOAP (http://sourceforge.net/projects/nusoap). There's no such need in PHP 5. In Chapter 12, you'll see just how easy these tasks are using the built-in SOAPClient class and SimpleXMLElement. Again it's the improved object model that makes this possible.

Reflection Classes

The reflection classes included in PHP 5 provide ways to introspect objects and reverse engineer code. The average web developer might be tempted to ignore these classes, but Chapter 14 shows how useful they are for automating a task that most developers approach with little enthusiasm: the creation of documentation.

Iterator

In addition to built-in classes, PHP 5 also offers built-in interfaces. Iterator is the most important, as a number of classes and interfaces are derived from this interface. I'll show you how to use Iterator in Chapter 10.

Backward Compatibility

Backward compatibility may be an issue if your code already uses objects. PHP 5 introduces a number of new "magic" methods. *Magic methods* begin with a double underscore, and this requires changing any user-defined methods or functions that use this naming convention. All of these methods will be discussed, particularly in Chapter 13. The most important ones relate to how objects are created and destroyed. The PHP 4 style of object creation is still supported, but you are encouraged to use the new magic method approach.

PHP 5 deprecates some existing object-related functions. For example, is_a has been replaced by a new operator, instanceof (see Chapter 14). This particular change won't affect how your code runs under PHP 5. If you use a deprecated function, you'll see a warning if the error-reporting level is set to E_STRICT (a useful technique for discovering where your code may need upgrading and discussed in more detail in Appendix A). In another example, the get_parent_class, get_class, and get_class_methods functions now return a case-sensitive result (though they don't require a case-sensitive parameter), so if you are using the returned result in a case-sensitive comparison you will have to make changes.

Pass By Reference

The preceding examples of changes are relatively minor and fairly easy to detect and upgrade. However, there is one change in particular that is of an entirely different magnitude.

The major change to PHP in version 5 relating to OOP is usually summed up by saying that objects are now passed by reference. This is true enough, but don't let this mask what's really at issue: a change in the way that the assignment operator works when used with objects.

Granted, the assignment operator is often invoked indirectly when an object is passed to a function or method, but objects are now passed by reference *because of* the implicit assignment. Prior to PHP 5, the default behavior was to assign objects by value and pass them to functions by value.

This is perfectly acceptable behavior for primitives, but it incurs far too much overhead with objects. Making a copy of a large object by passing it by value can put strains on memory and in most cases, all that's wanted is a reference to the original object rather than a copy. Changing the function of the assignment operator is a fairly significant change. In fact, the scripting engine that underlies PHP, the Zend engine, was entirely rewritten for PHP 5.

NOTE *In PHP 4 it's possible to pass objects by reference using the reference operator (&), and in fact it is good programming practice to do so. Needless to say, this use of the reference operator becomes entirely superfluous after upgrading to PHP 5. We'll discuss the implications of this change in Chapter 13, in the section "__clone" on page 116.*

Prognosis

The mere enumeration of the details of backward compatibility masks what can be a highly charged issue. Whenever you change an established language, there are competing interests. In many cases you're damned if you do and damned if you don't. For example, retaining inconsistent function naming conventions may be necessary to maintain backward compatibility, but you may also be criticized for this very lack of consistency.

Of course, breaking backward compatibility means that some existing code won't function properly. In many circumstances it's not easy to decide where and when to break backward compatibility, but changing PHP to pass objects by reference is a fairly defensible change despite any inconveniences. The only thing you can be sure of is that any change will give rise to complaints in some quarter. Certainly, having deprecated functions issue warnings is one good way to give advance notice and let developers prepare for coming changes.

Where to Go from Here

If you've bought this book and read this far you're obviously interested in OOP. If you know PHP already, then learning OO PHP will not be too difficult. Given the relative simplicity of PHP's object model, certainly less effort is required than for a C programmer to learn C++. Nevertheless, moving to a new language or a new version of a language entails some cost in terms of time and effort, especially if it has an impact on your existing code libraries.

We've covered some of the backward compatibility issues as they relate to OOP. Almost all procedural code will run with no changes under PHP 5. No rewrites are required, and code does not need to be converted to an OO style.

Upgrading existing applications to take advantage of PHP 5 is a different matter. In the case of some large applications, upgrading may require significant effort. Many applications will benefit by being upgraded. If you've ever tried to customize software such as phpBB (the popular open-source forum), you know that the task would be much simpler if the application was object-oriented. However, upgrading an application such as phpBB means beginning again from scratch.

And there are other considerations besides code compatibility. After learning the ins and outs of OOP with PHP 5, will you actually be able to make use of it? Are there actually servers out there running PHP 5?

Adoption of PHP 5

As of this writing PHP 5 is hardly a bleeding-edge technology. It has been available for more than a year, and there have been a number of bug fixes. It's a stable product. Where developers have control over web server configuration there's no question that upgrading to PHP 5 will be beneficial. But developers don't always have a choice in this matter. In some situations (where the developer has no control of the web host, for instance), the decision to upgrade is in someone else's hands.

PHP is a victim of its own success. The popularity and stability of PHP 4 have slowed the adoption of PHP 5. PHP 4 is a mature language that supports many applications, open-source and otherwise. There's naturally a reluctance to rock the boat. For this reason the adoption of PHP 5 has been somewhat slow, especially in shared hosting environments.

NOTE *Other web hosting options have been much quicker to adopt PHP 5. The various virtual private server (VPS) hosting options usually include PHP 5, as do dedicated hosts. As a more secure and increasingly inexpensive hosting option, VPS is becoming much more popular.*

Compromise

Widespread adoption of PHP 5 will happen sooner or later, but this book recognizes that developers may need, at least for a time, to continue writing new applications that will run under PHP 4. For this reason, wherever possible, a PHP 4 version of code has been provided in addition to the PHP 5 version.

In a sense, PHP 5 just formalizes what was already possible in PHP 4. For instance, even though PHP 4 allows direct access to instance variables, when creating a class in PHP 4 it makes sense to write accessor methods for variables rather than setting or retrieving them directly. This requires a disciplined approach, but it will yield code that not only runs under PHP 4 but also will be much easier to upgrade to PHP 5. Adding restrictive access modifiers to variables will be a relatively simple task if accessor methods are already in place. Writing code with the expectation of upgrading it will also invariably mean writing better code.

That's all the talk about OOP. In the remaining chapters you're going to do OOP.

4

SHOW A LITTLE CLASS

Introductory books on object-oriented programming (OOP) often use examples of objects taken from the real world. For example, you may be asked to imagine a "dog" class. We are all familiar with dogs, of course, so it's relatively easy to describe a dog's attributes. Most dogs have hair, four legs, and a tail. A dog's behavior is equally easy to describe. Dogs bark, jump, run, roll over, dig, and, when passing fire hydrants . . .

I don't mean to belittle this approach, but the objects that a web developer deals with are not often objects "out there" that one can point to. They are more likely to be conceptual rather than physical objects, and these are a little harder to identify. Once identified, it is not easy to describe the objects' attributes and behavior.

With that in mind, the class I propose you create is a list of files. (I know, it's not terribly exciting, but by keeping things simple, we can easily deal with some of the basic concepts of OOP.) This class certainly won't bark or jump, but by the time we're finished, it may roll over and do a few tricks.

NOTE *We'll use the syntax of PHP 4 to help ease into OOP. Starting with PHP 4 will also be helpful for those who have already used OOP with PHP and want to upgrade their code. I'll show you how to do this in Chapter 5, and for convenience, I have also included an appendix on this topic. (PHP 4 style code will run just fine under PHP 5 but will raise warnings if error reporting is set to E_STRICT in the php.ini file. See Appendix A for the OO configuration options of the php.ini file.)*

Design

OOP doesn't eliminate the need for systems analysis. It's easy to forget about this step and to just start coding, especially when dealing with a fairly simple task. However, a little forethought during the design stage will reap benefits later on, so make sure you have a clear idea of what you want to do.

Defining the Problem

You often need to look at and manipulate the files in a specific directory, and you often want to do this with directories that hold resources such as photos or images, .pdf files, or files that are compressed for downloading. Probably the simplest approach, if your web server is Apache, is not to use any code at all and simply put a .htaccess file containing the directive Options +Indexes into the appropriate directory.

By using a .htaccess file, you can simply point your browser to the directory that contains this file to see a list of its contents. Of course, if this were your only goal, then building a class to mimic this functionality would be entirely superfluous. However, you want to do a bit more than just list files. You want to have control over the order in which they appear and the file types that are listed, and you may also want to know the number of files.

Consider this fairly specific task: Suppose you have some cleanup work that needs doing on directories that contain graphics. You need to remove deadwood, but before you can do so, you need to view the images. Rather than open each picture individually using an application such as Photoshop or GIMP, you want to open all the files at once in your browser. Not only do you want to see the image, you also want to note the filename of the image in case you decide to remove it.

This is not a situation that requires an object-oriented (OO) solution. If you are familiar with PHP, you've probably already formulated a rough algorithm of how to solve this problem and determined which functions you need to use.

If you are a programmer but not familiar with OOP, a procedural approach will doubtless seem more natural and be easier to execute, especially when approaching a straightforward problem. However, remember that we are deliberately trying to keep things simple to begin with. Stick with me at least until the end of the next chapter—you won't be disappointed.

At this early stage, our simple class may not convince you of the utility of OOP, but it will highlight the fact that OOP doesn't do away with the need for procedural programming. The logic required for OOP is every bit as procedural as the functions you're used to creating and using.

Not the Da Vinci Code

We'll reproduce the code here and intersperse it with comments. (If you would like an overview of the entire class, now would be a good time to download the code for this chapter from the companion website at http://objectorientedphp.com.)

In order to create a class, use the keyword `class` and an appropriate name:

```
class DirectoryItems{ ... }
```

Braces enclose all the elements of a class, indicated by the ellipsis in the preceding line of code.

We discussed the concept of a class in Chapters 2 and 3, but a bit of repetition here won't be amiss. In its simplest form, a class can simply encapsulate a variety of data types, the way a `struct` does in C or a `type` in Visual Basic. This class will encapsulate data types, but it will also contain functions or methods.

Like PHP's built-in classes, we'll use Java-style naming conventions for the class name—not underscores, but uppercase letters for the start of each word, otherwise known as *studly caps*. We'll use the same naming convention for files that contain class definitions. For example, the file that holds the `DirectoryItems` class will be called `DirectoryItems.php`. This naming convention is not a requirement but helps readily identify classes and their files.

The first statement inside the class is the declaration of the variable `$filearray`. Upon declaration, this variable is initialized as an array.

```
var $filearray = array();
```

NOTE *Notice the use of the `var` keyword. This syntax will be replaced in PHP 5, but here it simply denotes an instance variable.*

Any variable declared at this level, namely inside the braces that enclose the class but outside any class function, is an *instance variable* or, as we might also refer to it, a *data member*. (In most cases, classes contain more than one data member, but one is sufficient for the moment.) Instance variables are sometimes also referred to as *properties*. The placement of instance variables outside of any function indicates that they have *scope* throughout the class. Their visibility is not restricted to any specific function—they can be accessed from anywhere within the class. You could say they are *global* to the class.

The Constructor

Next is a function that bears the same name as the class: the *constructor*. Constructors are commonly used to initialize data members, and as in Listing 4-1, filenames are added to the instance variable `$filearray`.

```
function DirectoryItems(❶$directory){
    $d = "";
    if(is_dir($directory)){
        $d = opendir($directory) or die("Couldn't open directory.");
```

```
        while(false !== ($f=readdir($d))){
            if(is_file("$directory/$f")){
                $this->❷filearray[] = $f;
            }
        }
        closedir($d);
    }else{
      //error
        die("Must pass in a directory.");
    }
}
```

Listing 4-1: The DirectoryItems constructor

Constructors are called whenever an object is created. In Listing 4-1, the constructor accepts, as a parameter, a string variable of ❶ a directory name. Any files contained within this directory are added to $filearray.

Referencing Instance Variables

The only remarkable thing about this code is the unusual syntax required to refer to the instance variable. Variables such as $d and $f, which are local to the constructor, are referenced in the same way as any other PHP variable, but when using ❷ $filearray, we must precede it with $this->.

If you're familiar with other OO languages such as C++ or Java, you'll be familiar with $this, a "pseudo-variable" that identifies what follows as an instance variable. However, unlike those other OO languages, use of $this when referring to an instance variable is not optional in PHP.

So much for the explanation of the syntax of the constructor. The constructor actually performs a fairly simple and straightforward programming task.

Wrapper Methods

The rest of the class is made up of a series of functions. Some of these functions simply enclose or wrap existing array-related functions and are called *wrapper functions*. These wrapper functions count or sort the list of filenames, but instead of calling them *functions*, let's use OO terminology and refer to them as *methods*.

NOTE   *When declaring the methods of a class you are required to use the keyword function. This can perhaps lead to some confusion. However, throughout we will use the term method to distinguish between a regular function call and the calling a class function.*

Again, following the studly caps naming convention, if a method name is a compound word, use lowercase for the first word and uppercase for any subsequent words. Listing 4-2 includes three methods that use built-in PHP array functions.

```
function indexOrder(){
    sort($this->filearray);
}
/////////////////////////////////////////////////////////////////////
function naturalCaseInsensitiveOrder(){
    natcasesort($this->filearray);
}
/////////////////////////////////////////////////////////////////////
function getCount(){
    return count($this->filearray);
}
```

Listing 4-2: Wrapper methods

Finally, add one final method to check that files are all images:

```
function checkAllImages(){
    $bln = true;
    $extension = "";
    $types = array(❶"jpg", "jpeg", "gif", "png");
    foreach ($this->filearray as $key => $value){
        $extension = substr($value,(strpos($value, ".") + 1));
        $extension = strtolower($extension);
        if(!in_array($extension, $types)){
            $bln = false;
            break;
        }
    }
    return $bln;
}
```

Listing 4-3: A method to select only images

The checkAllImages method loops through each element in the file array, extracts the extension, and checks that it is one of ❶ the acceptable file types.

In sum, the DirectoryItems class is made up of one data member, a special function called a constructor, and four other functions or methods. As already noted, you should save this file as DirectoryItems.php.

Creating an Instance

A class by itself is of absolutely no use whatsoever, and if you preview in a browser the code created so far, nothing will be displayed. That's because at this point we don't really have anything—just the idea for something. We need to create an *instance* of the class.

The many Platonists amongst you will immediately know what we're talking about. Remember Plato and "ideal forms?" Of course you do—it hasn't been that long since you took Philosophy 101. The explanation of a form usually involved a chair, because there was always one in the classroom. The form of a chair doesn't exist anywhere, but any specific chair embodies that form. In other words, each particular chair is an *instantiation* of the chair class. (If you skipped that lecture, we could say that a class acts as a template for a specific occurrence of a class in much the way that a building relates to its blueprint.)

Listing 4-4 is a PHP page that creates an instance of the DirectoryItems class. Briefly, this web page opens a directory immediately below the current working directory, checks that all the files in that directory are graphics files, sorts them in a case-insensitive way, and then displays them.

```html
<html>
<head>
<title>Images</title>
</head>
<body>
<?php
require ❶'DirectoryItems.php';
$di =& new DirectoryItems('graphics');
$di->checkAllImages() or die("Not all files are images.");
$di->❷naturalCaseInsensitiveOrder();
//get array
echo "<div style = \"text-align:center;\">";
foreach ($di->❸filearray as $key => $value){
    echo "<img src=\"graphics/$value\" /><br />\n";
}
echo "</div><br />";
?>
</body>
</html>
```

Listing 4-4: Creating an instance of the DirectoryItems class

Since we are going to create an instance of the DirectoryItems class, we need to include this class by requiring the file that holds ❶ the class definition, namely the file saved as DirectoryItems.php. We create the class instance with the code, $di =& new DirectoryItems('graphics');, where $di is the variable or instance of the object, and new both allocates memory and, in association with the class name, invokes the constructor. (When creating an object under PHP 4, it is advisable to return a reference using the assignment by reference operator, =&. The reason for this is discussed in detail in Chapter 13, in the section "__clone" on page 116.)

The constructor for the DirectoryItems class expects a directory name to be passed in. In this case, use graphics, which is assumed to be a directory immediately below the current directory. If the constructor cannot locate this directory, construction fails and the program terminates. But if it's successful, an array of filenames is created.

In this particular case we want to ensure that all the files in the graphics directory are images. After all, we're going to use this class to set the src attribute of an img tag. The checkAllImages method does this work by looking at filename extensions. The arrow operator we saw when using the pseudo-variable $this, reappears here when we want to call an object method: $di->checkAllImages().

Calling an object method is similar to calling a function in procedural programming. However, instead of passing a variable to a function as is commonly done, a class method is called on a variable, or more properly speaking, an object or instance of a class. This is how objects may be said to *behave*: they *do* things rather than having things done to them.

Next, perform ❷ a case-insensitive sort of the filenames. Directly access the data member, ❸ $filearray, and iterate through this array to display each image.

As you can see, we've created a class and used it to accomplish exactly what we set out to do.

What Have You Accomplished?

Using the syntax of PHP 4, you have created a class to assist in the display of images in a web page. It is a fairly simple class, and it should be readily apparent how the same job could be done procedurally.

However, despite the simplicity of the class and of the task it performs, there are some obvious advantages. On the plus side, you could say the HTML page is fairly clean—the somewhat messy task of determining if all files are image files has been hidden away inside the class file. Additionally, if you want to reuse this code, you won't have to cut and paste the way you so often do with procedural programming; you need only use the require directive with the class filename, and away you go.

But would you want to reuse this class? Skeptics might say that we've come the long way around and built a class to solve a specific problem, but that we could have achieved the same effect more quickly using procedural programming. Additionally, they might argue that this class is just an ad hoc solution not easily reused elsewhere.

There may be some truth to these criticisms; certainly the more a class is tied to the specifics of a situation, the less reusable it is. However, remember that we set out to create a fairly simple class with the intention of elucidating some of the basics of OO programming. At this point we only have a fledgling class that requires more nurturing.

But Will It Fly?

OO enthusiasts are usually eager to point out the big ways in which OOP is superior to procedural programming, through capabilities such as inheritance, for instance. True enough, but probably of more importance is the fact that once you have a class, providing that the basic design is sound, you can easily add to its functionality. If it doesn't do something you want it to do, the simplest and often the best solution is to add a method to create additional behavior.

For example, you could easily add a method modeled on the method checkAllImages that would check for other types of files. Or, suppose some of the files in the directory passed to the constructor are not image files, and you don't want your program to attempt to display them. This could be remedied with a filter method. I'm sure you can think of other ways in which this class can be improved. The next chapter will improve on this class so that it can be used in a variety of ways, but the focus will be on its use with a directory of image files.

Furthermore, some of the shortcomings of this class suggest the creation of additional classes rather than additions to the DirectoryItems class. First, images are of varying sizes. This not only affects the aesthetics of a web page, but, if the images are large, this can significantly slow the rate at which a page downloads. Second, if there are a considerable number of files in one directory, a single web page that displays all of them will be unacceptably long. In later chapters we'll follow up on both of these ideas.

At the beginning of this chapter I promised that we wouldn't create a dog class, and perhaps instead, we've created an ugly duckling. In any case, you'll want to stick around for another chapter not only to see if our fledgling can fly but also to see whether our ugly duckling turns into a swan.

5

MOD UR CLASS

Chapter 4 left us with some clear objectives. We need to add functionality to the `DirectoryItems` class, and we need to upgrade it to take advantage of the changes introduced in PHP 5. And that's exactly what we'll do in this chapter. We'll upgrade the syntax of the `DirectoryItems` class first; then we'll improve its functionality by adding methods.

Keeping in mind that we plan to use the `DirectoryItems` class to display images, we'll add a method that ignores all non-image files, so we don't need to worry if other file types occur within a directory containing mostly images. We'll also broaden the scope of the class so that we can filter the contents of a directory and focus on a specific file type.

Upgrading to PHP 5

As you're aware, the major change to PHP with version 5 is improved support for OOP. In this regard, two of the most important changes are the introduction of access modifiers and changed syntax for class construction. Both of these changes will have an impact on the `DirectoryItems` class.

Access Modifiers

Next to the concept of a class, *access modifiers* are arguably the most important feature of an OO language. The principal use of access modifiers is to describe and constrain data members and methods. The access modifiers we are concerned with in this chapter are `public` and `private`. The modifier `private` is used to modify or describe matters relating to the internal behavior of a class. The modifier `public` is used to describe the external behavior of a class or, if you prefer, a class's interface.

As far as syntactic changes to the `DirectoryItems` class are concerned, this means replacing the keyword `var` with `private`, so that

```
var $filearray = array();
```

becomes

```
private $filearray = array();
```

As you'll recall, `$filearray` is the sole data member of the `DirectoryItems` class. In most cases (except static classes, which we will discuss in Chapter 11), you should make all data members private, because by doing so, you are protecting the integrity of your data by restricting access to it.

To better understand access modifiers, it's useful to think of data members or instance variables as though they are data in a database. In order to maintain the integrity of the data in a database, it's wise to limit access and restrict the ways in which data can be added or changed. A programmer might well write an application to achieve this result, requiring users to log in and implementing controls on the way in which data are formatted. For instance, you may want dates stored in a particular format and enforce this through the use of a masked textbox.

Since access modifiers are nonexistent in PHP 4, changing the value of a variable only requires a simple assignment. You could modify the `$filearray` variable in the following way:

```
$di->filearray[0] = "anyfile.jpg";
```

It's a disadvantage to do things this way because changes to `$filearray` are not controlled and allowing direct access to data members greatly increases the risk of contaminating your data. If you use the keyword `private`, direct access is no longer possible.

NOTE   *In terms of the preceding database analogy, making an instance variable private means that access to the data is only permitted through use of the programmer's application or front end.*

But wait, it's your code, right? You won't change it improperly, so why should you care? Because OO programming assumes that other programmers may use your objects and vice versa.

Bruce Eckel refers to this as *client programmers* using objects created by *class creators.*[1] Even if you are a lone developer and don't expect other programmers to use your code, access modifiers are still an important safeguard. Why? How many times have you returned to your own code, even after only a short period of time away from it, and had trouble trying to figure out what exactly you were trying to achieve? Clearly, in this situation, even though you are the class originator, you are also, at the same time, a client programmer. The use of access modifiers forces the programmer to make his or her intentions explicit. If a particular data member or method relates to the internal behavior of a class, then applying the appropriate access modifier documents this intention. If nothing else, we all need access modifiers to protect our code from that most presumptuous of client programmers—ourselves.

When first encountering the private keyword, there is sometimes a mistaken tendency to view it solely as a security measure and then point out its ineffectiveness by showing how easily a malicious user programmer could subvert it. Even more so with a non-compiled language like PHP, because it's an easy matter to change a modifier from private to public. It's better to view the use of access modifiers as indicative of the originating programmer's intentions—as a form of internal documentation. (However, the use of access modifiers does add to security insofar as any well thought out and well documented class is a more secure class.)

The private keyword can be applied to methods as well as to data members. You'll see an example of a private method later in this chapter, but for the moment, let's look at the use of the modifier public when applied to a method.

Once the need for the keyword private is apparent, so also is the need for a public method or interface so that private data members may be accessed in a controlled fashion. Now that the $filearray variable is private, you no longer have *any* kind of access to it. For this reason, you need a public method, sometimes called an *accessor method*, in order to retrieve that private variable:

```
public function getFileArray(){
    return $this->filearray
}
```

In the previous chapter, you directly accessed this data member thus: $di->filearray. You might well wonder what the difference is and conclude that direct access is preferable because it is more succinct. However, the important difference is that when you directly access a data member, you are working

---

[1] Bruce Eckel, *Thinking in Java* (Prentice Hall, 1998), 30.

with the original, but when you use a method to retrieve a data member, you retrieve a *copy* of that original. When working directly with the original, you risk changing its value, inadvertently or otherwise. When working with a copy, there is no such danger because, should the copy be changed, the original will remain intact. In other words, what's returned from the getFileArray method is returned by value, not by reference. Changing the copy won't have any effect on the original.

It is perhaps clearer now how a public method is an interface. A public method mediates between a data member and a user programmer in the same way that the front end of a database mediates between a user and the data. Controlled access to the data simplifies how a class is used and, in so doing, helps preserve its integrity.

The Constructor

In Chapter 4, you saw how the class name functioned as a special method called the *constructor*. However, PHP 5 changes the way that objects are constructed. Specifically,

```
function DirectoryItems($directory){ ... }
```

becomes

```
public function __construct($directory){ ... }
```

Methods beginning with a double underscore are *magic methods*. They are given this name because they are not (usually) called directly. This new method for constructing objects is invoked in exactly the same way as a constructor is invoked under PHP 4. Creating an instance of the DirectoryItems class still uses the keyword new along with the class name:

```
$di = new DirectoryItems("graphics");
```

The syntax for creating an object is the same, but in PHP 5, the __construct method is executed rather than a method bearing the class name.

NOTE   *In PHP 5, you need not return the object created by the constructor (or any method for that matter) by reference. The reason for this is explained in Chapter 13 in the section "__clone" on page 116.*

Altering the constructor may seem like an unnecessary change to those of you familiar with constructors in other OO languages, but there are advantages that you'll see when we discuss inheritance. Without getting into the details of inheritance at this early stage, let's just say that having a fixed name for the constructor in every class allows you to avoid hard-coding class names unnecessarily. This in turn will of course make your code easier to maintain.

NOTE   *The access modifier public is optional when applied to a constructor (or any other method, for that matter), but it certainly doesn't hurt to use it. You may still create a constructor using the class name, but adopting the style of PHP 5 now will avoid any future backward-compatibility issues.*

Modifying Your Class

You've upgraded the syntax of your code to PHP 5 standards, but you still need to improve the functionality of your DirectoryItems class. This involves rewriting the constructor to make it do a bit more work and adding more methods to the class. The additional methods will improve the flexibility of the class by filtering for specific file types.

Reconstructing the Constructor

Currently, the constructor for the DirectoryItems class uses an array to keep track of filenames. The underutilization of the capabilities of an array suggest changes to the constructor.

Arrays in PHP are very flexible—they can be either numerical or associative. The current constructor simply stores the filenames in a numeric array, but if you change this to an associative array, you can make better use of the data member $filearray. Since all operating systems require that each filename within a directory be unique, the filename is ideal for acting as a key in an associative array. Let's see how you might take advantage of this.

When properly ordered and created, a directory and its subdirectories can function like a database and its tables; in fact, for some databases, a table *is* a directory and its contents.

If you consider the DirectoryItems class as a table and the files in the array as "records," then, if you set things up in just the right way, filenames can function as the "title" field for each file in that database.

You can implement this by using a strict naming convention for all your files. For example, if all your files are formatted using underscores to separate words (Lady_of_Shallott.jpg, for instance), then by replacing underscores with spaces and stripping out filename extensions, the filename alone can serve as the title for each image when it is displayed.

I won't reproduce the original code for the constructor here, but look back at Chapter 4 if you need to refresh your memory. The code for the new constructor and a private method called from within the constructor is shown in Listing 5-1.

```
public function __construct($directory, ❶$replacechar = "_"){
    $this->directory = $directory;
    $this->❷replacechar=$replacechar;
    $d = "";
    if(is_dir($directory)){
        $d = opendir($directory) or die("Failed to open directory.");
        while(false !== ($f=readdir($d))){
            if(is_file("$directory/$f")){
                $title = $this->❸createTitle($f);
                $this->filearray[$f] = $title;
            }
        }
        closedir($d);
    }else{
        //error
```

```
                        die("Must pass in a directory.");
                }
        }
❹private function createTitle($title){
                //strip extension
                $title = substr($title,0,strrpos($title, "."));
                //replace word separator
                $title = str_replace($this->replacechar," ",$title);
                return $title;
        }
```

Listing 5-1: The constructor and the createTitle method

The original constructor for this class accepted only one parameter—a directory name. You are now passing an additional parameter, ❶ $replacechar, and it has a default value of "_". This parameter will function as the character in a filename and will be replaced by a space in order to make a readable, English "title" from the filename.

By assigning a default value to $replacechar, users of the DirectoryItems class have three options. They can:

1. Use another replacement character by passing a second value to the constructor (a hyphen, perhaps)

2. Let the second value default to an underscore

3. Simply ignore the existence of this parameter (if they don't want to use a title)

Next, you copy the character used as a word separator into ❷ an instance variable, because you need to reference it not only in the constructor but also in the createTitle method.

In the original version of this class, you did not need to keep track of the directory name passed to the constructor because once it was used in the constructor, it was no longer needed. Because you intend to filter filenames, you now need to preserve the directory name, so you copy it into an instance variable. How you use the variable $directory will become apparent when we discuss the removeFilter method later in this chapter.

NOTE   *Local variables can have the same name as instance variables because the pseudo-variable $this allows you to distinguish one from the other.*

The method createTitle (❸) creates the title for each image by removing the filename extension and replacing the underscores with spaces. This method is reproduced in full starting at ❹.

Notice the use of ❹ the access modifier private. This method, the only private method in the entire class, is private because there is no reason to access it except from the constructor. The createTitle method affects the internal behavior of the DirectoryItems class and identifying it as private allows you to indicate that this behavior is internal and hidden rather than external and exposed.

To briefly return to our earlier discussion of access modifiers, another way of describing the difference between public and private access, as far as methods are concerned, is to say that they separate the interface from the implementation. A user programmer need only concern himself with the public methods of a class in order to use it efficiently. In other words, he need not worry about private functions because they represent the inner workings of a class's implementation. For this reason, you can say that the separation of public and private methods simplifies the use of a class.

In the original version of the constructor presented in Chapter 4, you assigned each filename to an array element, effectively creating a numeric array. In the revised constructor, however, you have created an associative array, with the filename functioning as the *key* and the title as the *value*. As noted earlier, you can't have files in the same directory with duplicate names, so the filename can function as a unique key.

Filtering Content

To this point, you have changed the DirectoryItems class to take advantage of changes to the syntax of PHP, namely by using access modifiers and the "magic" constructor. You've also changed the internal workings of the constructor in order to create a "title." All that remains is to create the methods that relate to filtering the contents of a directory.

However, there's no point in filtering if you don't have to; a directory may already contain only the file type you are interested in. Hence, you need a method to loop through all files and determine whether they are the same type. Listing 5-2 contains this method.

```
public function checkAllSpecificType(❶$extension){
    $extension = strtolower($extension);
    $bln = true;
    $ext = "";
    foreach ($this->filearray as $key => $value){
        $ext = substr($key,(strpos($key, ".") + 1));
        $ext = strtolower($ext);
        if($extension != $ext){
            $bln = false;
            break;
        }
    }
    return $bln;
}
```

Listing 5-2: The checkAllSpecificType method

Listing 5-2 is a simple modification of the method developed in Chapter 4—checkAllImages. You can check that a directory contains only a specific file type by passing ❶ an $extension to this method. For instance, you can determine if a directory holds only Portable Document Format (PDF) files by passing the value pdf to this method. This method returns true if all file extensions in this directory match pdf.

But in the real world, things aren't usually quite so tidy. Often a directory holds a variety of file types. If you call the method checkAllSpecificType and it returns false, you know you need to filter the contents of a directory, and that's what the code in Listing 5-3 does.

```php
public function filter($extension){
    $extension = strtolower($extension);
    foreach ($this->filearray as $key => $value){
        $ext = substr($key,(strpos($key, ".")+1));
        $ext = strtolower($ext);
        if($ext != $extension){
            ❶unset ($this->filearray[$key]);
        }
    }
}
```

Listing 5-3: The filter method

If you use the example of Portable Document Format files again, passing the file extension pdf to the filter method removes all other files from $filearray. This is done by looping through the array and ❶ unsetting elements that don't match. If there are a variety of files in a directory and you invoke the filter method, you no longer have a complete list of files.

While this isn't going to be a problem in some situations, suppose you have a mixture of .pdf files and images in a specific directory and you want to download all the .pdf files and after that, display all the images. Once you have filtered for .pdf files, you need to reset the file array to its original values so that you can view the images. You need a method to remove the filter from a directory.

Resetting the Array

An alternative to resetting the file array would be to construct another instance of the DirectoryItems object. The less radical approach, shown in Listing 5-4, is to remove the filter.

```php
public function removeFilter(){
    unset($this->❶filearray);
    $d = "";
    $d = opendir($this->❷directory) or die("Couldn't open directory.");
    while(false !== ($f = readdir($d))){
        if(is_file("$this->directory/$f")){
            $title = $this->createTitle($f);
            $this->filearray[$f] = $title;
        }
    }
    closedir($d);
}
```

Listing 5-4: The removeFilter method

This removeFilter method first empties (unsets) ❶ the $filearray variable and then repeats the process that occurred in the constructor; namely, it recreates the $filearray variable.

As mentioned earlier when discussing the constructor, the original version of this class discarded the directory name after it was used in the constructor. It's now apparent that you need this value because you may have to reconstruct ❷ the file array from scratch.

You have an existing method—checkAllImages—that reports whether all the files within a directory are image files, but you also require a method that filters out all non-image files. The checkAllSpecificType method won't do because it filters for one extension only, and there are a variety of different extensions for image files. Hence the need for the imagesOnly method in Listing 5-5 that removes all non-image files from the array instance variable.

```php
public function imagesOnly(){
    $extension = "";
    ❶$types = array("jpg", "jpeg", "gif", "png");
    foreach($this->filearray as $key => $value){
        $extension = substr($key,(strpos($key, ".") + 1));
        $extension = strtolower($extension);
        if(!in_array($extension, $types)){
            unset($this->filearray[$key]);
        }
    }
}
```

Listing 5-5: The imagesOnly method

This code performs exactly the same function as the checkAllSpecificType method, but it retains files with the four different extensions associated with images rather than just one file type. This is done by looping through all the filenames, extracting the extension and examining whether it appears in ❶ the $types array. Again, to restore the file array to its original state, use the removeFilter method.

Summary of Changes

In this chapter, we've built upon the simple DirectoryItems class that was introduced in Chapter 4 to produce an expanded and upgraded class. As you've seen, you needed to make surprisingly few changes to this class in order to implement some of the key changes introduced with PHP 5.

Certainly, the changes described in this chapter are not the only changes to PHP's OO capabilities; however, one of them—the use of access modifiers—is possibly the most important. The single most glaring shortcoming of OO programming in PHP 4 is this lack of access modifiers. While disciplined use and careful documentation can take you part of the way toward mitigating this deficiency, it's much better to rely on the structure of the language to enforce the appropriate use of an object.

Not only have you upgraded the DirectoryItems class, but you've also expanded its functionality with a view to using it to display a series of images. The ugly duckling class is well on its way to becoming a full-fledged swan.

The DirectoryItems class was created in order to display a directory of images. Further changes are needed to perform this task properly but these changes require the creation of additional classes. In Chapter 6 let's look at creating a thumbnail image class to produce thumbnails of images.

6

THE THUMBNAILIMAGE CLASS

Images are often of unequal dimensions, and their file sizes can vary greatly. This inconsistency creates problems when downloading and displaying a group of images because one large image can take up the entire screen, dwarfing smaller images. Also, if image files are large, they can slow downloading to an unacceptable pace.

One solution to the problem of inconsistently sized images is to create a thumbnail image class, which creates small images (thumbnails) of equal size. By reducing the quality of an image, this class will be able to further reduce file size and hence download times.

Since we intend to use the DirectoryItems class with directories of images, this additional supporting class takes the next step toward improving the utility of the DirectoryItems class. Furthermore, developing this class should give you a good idea of when a method should be private, how to limit access to data members with set and get methods, how to set default values for data members upon declaration, and how to ensure that resources are disposed of properly.

What Does a Designer Do?

To determine what the `DirectoryItems` class should do, consider how web designers create thumbnail images. They typically open an image file in a graphic editor, reduce its dimensions (and perhaps its quality), and then resave the file under a different name.

For ease of placement on the screen, images in a group are usually reduced to approximately the same thumbnail size as each other. In other words, the thumbnail for a large image is roughly the same size as the thumbnail for a medium-sized image. The image is typically reduced to a predetermined maximum dimension while constraining its proportions so as not to distort it. This maximum dimension is usually applied to the width or the height, depending upon whether the image's orientation is landscape or portrait. While this maximum will vary, the maximum size of a thumbnail should be such that it is small enough to download quickly, but large enough for the viewer to form an accurate impression of the full-sized picture. Once created, the thumbnail is typically displayed in a web page, where it might function as a hyperlink to its full-sized counterpart.

Mimicking the Designer

Having considered how the web designer handles thumbnails, we can better determine how a thumbnail class should behave. We will build a class that mimics the way a designer creates a thumbnail but with certain improvements.

When the designer creates a thumbnail, he writes a separate file to disk. While it might make sense in some cases for a class to create thumbnail images only once and then save them to disk, we will create them on the fly, as needed, and output them to the browser without saving them. This approach allows us to create a simpler, and in some respects, a more flexible class. We won't have to worry about where to store the thumbnails or whether a thumbnail has already been created for a specific image.

NOTE *The downside to this approach is that it requires more server-side processing, and, if there are a large number of images per web page, it may degrade server performance. We'll solve this problem in Chapter 7.*

Help from PHP Functions

When creating the thumbnail image class, the equivalent of the designer's graphic editor is the existing PHP image function library, which contains the tools you need to manipulate common image types. PHP's `imagecreatefrom` functions return a resource making it possible to programmatically copy an image, reduce its dimensions, and also reduce its quality if necessary.

Thus, you have your editor and you know how your class should behave. You know too that you want to preserve the proportions of an image when you create a thumbnail and that you want to reduce all images to the same approximate thumbnail size. You're all set to start coding.

The ThumbnailImage Class

In the following sections, you'll examine the entire ThumbnailImage class, interspersing the code with comments.

Data Members

As always, the data members are private. The variable $image holds the actual thumbnail image itself.

```
private $image;
private $quality = 100;
private $mimetype;
private $imageproperties = array();
private $initialfilesize;
```

Since, in some cases, you may want to vary the quality of the thumbnail, you create the attribute $quality. For very large files (large in terms of byte count rather than just dimensions), you may need to reduce the quality of an image as well as its size. Give $quality a default value of 100 to indicate no reduction in quality, because in most cases, you will retain the quality of the original image.

NOTE *The assignment of a value to* $quality *shows that data members may be initialized upon declaration, but they must be initialized with constant values. You could not, for instance, invoke a PHP function call or a method.*

If you are going to output an image, you need to know whether it's a .jpeg, .gif, or .png file, hence the need for a MIME type attribute. Finally, add $imageproperties, principally to capture the dimensions of the original image. Initialize it as an array (although there is no requirement to do so), because doing so is a nice way to document the data type of this variable.

NOTE *Knowing the MIME type makes it easier for the browser to display an image.*

Deconstructing the Constructor

As you saw in Chapter 5, the constructor is a magic method that begins with a double underscore and is invoked whenever a new instance of a class is created. The constructor for the ThumbnailImage class is shown in Listing 6-1.

```
public function❺ __construct($file, $thumbnailsize = 100){
    //check file
```

```
❶is_file($file) or die ("File: $file doesn't exist.");
$this->initialfilesize = filesize($file);
$this->imageproperties = getimagesize($file) or die ("Incorrect file_
type.");
    // new function image_type_to_mime_type
$this->mimetype = ❷image_type_to_mime_type($this->imageproperties[2]);
    //create image
switch($this->imageproperties[2]){
    case IMAGETYPE_JPEG:
        $this->image = ❸imagecreatefromJPEG($file);
        break;
    case IMAGETYPE_GIF:
        $this->image = imagecreatefromGIF($file);
        break;
    case IMAGETYPE_PNG:
        $this->image = imagecreatefromPNG($file);
        break;
    default:
        die("Couldn't create image.");
}
❹$this->createThumb($thumbnailsize);
}
```

Listing 6-1: The constructor for the ThumbnailImage class

The code first checks that ❶ the $file passed in is legitimate, and, if so, it retrieves the properties of the image. In addition to file dimensions, the built-in PHP function filesize returns a constant integer that indicates the file's MIME type. This PHP constant can be converted to a string value by using ❷ the image_type_to_mime_type function.

NOTE   *This function is new to PHP 5, so if you are working in PHP 4, the code needs to be different. This work has been done for you. Download the version 4 files of Chapter 6 to see how the same results are achieved by looking at file extensions. Knowing the MIME type will be necessary when you want to output your image.*

The appropriate, image-specific imagecreatefrom function (❸) is called and a resource is returned. The actual thumbnail is created by manipulating this resource in ❹ the createThumb method.

Two parameters are passed to ❺ the constructor. The parameter $file is required; $thumbnailsize is optional because it has a default value. The $file variable tells your class where to find the image that is to be reduced, and $thumbnailsize indicates the dimension that it will be reduced to.

Two Ways to Construct an Object

When discussing constructors in Chapter 5, you saw how default values can be assigned to parameters, thus providing flexibility and improving ease of use. The assignment of the value 100 to the variable $thumbnailsize means that the default size of your thumbnail will be 100 pixels.

Because this variable has a default value, you can create a class instance in two different ways. To accept the default thumbnail size, create an object like so:

```
$thumb = new ThumbnailImage("graphics/My_Picture.jpg");
```

In this case, the maximum dimension of the thumbnail will be the default value.

To construct a thumbnail of different dimensions, do the following:

```
$thumb = new ThumbnailImage("graphics/My_Picture.jpg", 250);
```

Assigning a default value to an argument to the constructor is simply a convenience for users of your class.

NOTE *When assigning default values to arguments to a method, you may have as many default values as you wish. However, arguments without a default value should not follow those that have a default value; in this particular class, the $path variable should not follow the $thumbnailsize variable.*

Internal Behavior—Private Methods

So far you have seen only private data members, but here you encounter your first private method. Private methods relate to the internal workings of a class and can be invoked only from within the class itself. The method that performs the image reduction (see Listing 6-2) is a private method—createThumb—called from within the constructor.

```
private function createThumb($thumbnailsize){
    //array elements for width and height
    $srcW = $this->imageproperties[0];
    $srcH = $this->imageproperties[1];
    //only adjust if larger than max
    if($srcW > $thumbnailsize || $srcH ❶> $thumbnailsize){
        $reduction = $this->calculateReduction($thumbnailsize);
        //get proportions
        $desW = $srcW/$reduction;
        $desH = $srcH/$reduction;
        $copy = imagecreatetruecolor($desW, $desH);
        imagecopyresampled($copy,$this->image,0,0,0,0,$desW, $desH, $srcW,
$srcH) or die ("Image copy failed.");
        //destroy original
        imagedestroy($this->image);
        ❷$this->image = $copy;
    }
}
```

Listing 6-2: The createThumb method

In this listing, createThumb checks the width and height of the image to determine whether ❶ it is greater than the targeted size. If it is, the method creates a reduced copy and ❷ overwrites the original image with the copy.

This private method for image reduction is called from the constructor and may only be invoked from within the class. By calling it from within the constructor, it need not be called directly, and the client programmer benefits by having a fully-formed and usable object immediately upon construction.

Must It Be Private?

Suppose for a moment, though, that your intention was to make a number of different-sized reductions of the same image, just as a photographer often makes different-sized copies of the same picture. In this case, it might make sense to save the original image and make the createThumb method public. As such, an image could be recreated at different sizes by repeatedly calling this method and passing the method different values.

In fact, with minimal change to the code and the interface, you could make your class accommodate this scenario and still fulfill its original intention.

A Helper Method

From within the createThumb method, you call another private method, calculateReduction, shown in Listing 6-3.

```
private function calculateReduction($thumbnailsize){
    $srcW = $this->imageproperties[0];
    $srcH = $this->imageproperties[1];
    //adjust
    if($srcW < $srcH){
        $reduction = round($srcH/$thumbnailsize);
    }else{
        $reduction = round($srcW/$thumbnailsize);
    }
    return $reduction;
}
```

Listing 6-3: The calculateReduction method

The calculateReduction method determines whether the height or width of the image is larger and then calculates the percentage reduction based on the targeted thumbnail size. In other words, it determines whether the image's orientation is landscape or portrait and reduces the image on the appropriate dimension.

NOTE   *Unlike the createThumb method, the calculateReduction method is inherently private. It is a helper method that returns the percentage reduction to the createThumb method.*

Public Methods

Following the constructor is another public method with the name __destruct. This method is known as a *destructor*. The double underscore (__) in front of the function name indicates that this method, like the constructor, is another magic method. Again, it is a method newly introduced in PHP 5. (Recall from Chapter 5 that magic methods happen in the background, like magic.)

```
public function __destruct(){
    if(isset($this->image)){
        imagedestroy($this->image);
    }
}
```

While the use of destructors is new with PHP 5, anyone familiar with other OO languages has probably already come across them. As its name suggests, a destructor is the opposite of a constructor. A constructor initializes an object, while a destructor frees up resources that a class may have allocated. Generally, PHP does a good job of cleaning up after itself so destructors are often not strictly necessary. It's used here to ensure that the image resource is disposed of.

Garbage Collection

Like Java, PHP employs a garbage collector to automatically clean up resources. Because the programmer is not responsible for allocating and freeing memory (as he is in a language like C++, for example), an automated program must free up resources. The garbage collector determines when objects are no longer used and then disposes of them, for example, when they go out of scope. However, using destructors can act as a cue that speeds up garbage collection. In the case of the ThumbnailImage class, the destructor disposes of the reduced image copy by calling the imagedestroy function.

You can call the destructor directly but, as with other magic methods the destructor is designed to be invoked in the background without any intervention by the programmer.

Displaying the Image

Next to the constructor, getImage (see Listing 6-4) is the most important method in the ThumbnailImage class, because it actually sends a reduced image to the browser. Its logic is simple: A header is sent to the browser announcing what to expect, followed by the appropriate content.

```
public function getImage(){
    header("Content-type: $this->mimetype");
    switch($this->imageproperties[2]){
```

```
        case IMAGETYPE_JPEG:
            imagejpeg($this->image, "", ❶$this->quality);
            break;
        case IMAGETYPE_GIF:
            imagegif($this->image);
            break;
        case IMAGETYPE_PNG:
            imagepng($this->image, "", ❶$this->quality);
            break;
        default:
            die("Couldn't create image.");
    }
}
```

Listing 6-4: The getImage method

Because .png and .jpeg image types support a reduction in quality, ❶ the quality argument is included when the images are output. The proper MIME type is sent to the browser first, and subsequently the image is sent in binary format.

Get and Set Methods

Chapter 5 introduced the concept of private data members and discussed how they create a need for accessor methods (also referred to as get and set methods), which retrieve and change the value of data members. The getMimeType method retrieves the MIME type of your thumbnail image. (Recall that the value returned is a copy and not the original.)

```
public function getMimeType(){
    return $this->mimetype;
}
```

You need to retrieve the value of the private variable mimetype when you display your thumbnail. Merely retrieving the MIME type can do no harm, but the same cannot be said of setting this value. The MIME type is set in the constructor by looking at an image's properties. Since this information can be determined programmatically and since an image's MIME type does not change, there is no need to set this value. Hence, there is no set method to match the get method. To say the same thing in another way, $mimetype is a read-only value and having only a get method contributes to data protection.

Image Quality

On the other hand, it makes sense to have both a set and get method for image quality. The quality property of a ThumbnailImage object is quite different from an image's MIME type and is not something that must remain fixed. In fact, getting and setting the quality of an image is one of the requirements that you set out to achieve when you designed this class. Let's first look at the method that sets image quality in Listing 6-5.

```
public function setQuality($quality){
    if❶($quality > 100 || $quality <  1){
        $quality = 75;
        ❷if($this->imageproperties[2] == IMAGETYPE_JPEG || $this-
>imageproperties[2] == IMAGETYPE_PNG){
    $this->quality = $quality;
    }
}
```

Listing 6-5: The setQuality method

As you can see in this listing, ❶ negative values and values greater
than 100 are prohibited because they are not valid values for image quality.
Furthermore, .gif images don't support alterations of the image quality, so
❷ the second if statement checks for the appropriate image type before
changing the quality. A set method is superior to direct access to an object's
properties because values can be tested and rejected, if need be, before they
are assigned. A set method allows you to restrict how the variable quality is
changed by screening out illegal values.

While the need to control the way in which object properties are
changed is somewhat obvious, retrieving object properties through an
accessor method is also superior to directly accessing a public data member.
Because you can't alter the quality of a GIF, there is no need to retrieve it,
and the getQuality method (see Listing 6-6) reflects this.

```
public function getQuality(){
    $quality = null;
    if($this->imageproperties[2] == ❶IMAGETYPE_JPEG || $this-
>imageproperties[2] == IMAGETYPE_PNG){
        $quality = $this->quality;
    }
    return $quality;
}
```

Listing 6-6: The getQuality method

Just as the setQuality method restricted changes to the quality of a .gif
image, the getQuality method only returns a legitimate value if ❶ the image
is a .jpeg or .png. Otherwise, null is returned.

Accessor methods are superior to direct access to public data members
because they restrict how a variable is changed and how it is retrieved. They
help ensure the integrity of your data and the functionality of the class as a
whole. Get and set methods allow you to ignore the fact that .gif images don't
support a quality attribute in a way that unfettered public access cannot.

When to Change the Quality

In order to determine if the quality of an image needs reducing, it's helpful
to know a bit more about the image. The getInitialFileSize function returns
the image's original size in bytes. This information helps you decide whether
to reduce the quality of an image and, if so, by how much.

```
public function getInitialFileSize(){
    return $this->initialfilesize;
}
```

The code in this chapter doesn't actually call this method, but you can imagine the circumstances in which it might be useful.

Displaying a Thumbnail

The process of outputting a series of thumbnail images to the browser occurs in two steps. First, you create a script that outputs an image; then you use this script file as the source for an img tag.

The code in Listing 6-7 shows the script file for outputting an image. It retrieves the path and size from a query string and uses these values to construct a thumbnail and then display it (in this chapter's downloads, this is the file getthumb.php).

```
<?php
//this file will be the src for an img tag
require 'ThumbnailImage.php';
$path = $_GET["path"];
$maxsize = @$_GET["size"];
if(!isset($maxsize)){
    $maxsize = 100;
}
if(isset($path)){
    $thumb = new ThumbNailImage($path, $maxsize);
    ❶$thumb->getImage();
}
?>
```

Listing 6-7: Constructing and displaying a thumbnail image

When passed a query string describing the path to an image file and the desired image size, this code outputs a thumbnail directly to the browser. The getImage method (❶) tells the browser the MIME type to expect and then sends the image file in binary format.

NOTE   *Typing getthumb.php?path=graphics/filename.jpg into the browser address bar is equivalent to pointing your browser directly at an image file. However, because you want to output a series of pictures and control their position, you will use this file as the src attribute of an img tag.*

Putting It All Together

The short piece of code in Listing 6-8 uses the DirectoryItems class together with the ThumbnailImage class to display all images within a directory, at reduced sizes.

```
<?php
require 'DirectoryItems.php';
```

```
$dc = ❶new DirectoryItems('graphics');
$dc->imagesOnly();
$dc->naturalCaseInsensitiveOrder();
$path = "";
$filearray = $dc->getFileArray();
echo "<div style=\"text-align:center;\">";
echo "Click the filename to view full-sized version.<br />";
//specify size of thumbnail
$size = 100;
foreach ($filearray as $key => $value){
    $path = "graphics/".$key;
    /*errors in getthumb or in class will result in broken links
    - error will not display*/
    echo "<img ❷src=\"getthumb.php?path=$path&amp;size=$size\" ".
        "style=\"border:1px solid black;margin-top:20px;\" ".
        "alt= \"$value\" /><br />\n";
    echo "<a href=\"$path\" target=\"_blank\" >";
    echo "Title: $value</a> <br />\n";
}
echo "</div><br />";
?>
```

Listing 6-8: Displaying all the images in a directory at reduced size

As shown in Listing 6-8, you first construct ❶ a DirectoryItems object and pass it the directory named graphics. You filter non-image files with the imagesOnly function, and the path is passed as a query string to the getthumb.php file, which, in turn, is assigned to ❷ the src attribute of an img tag.

This may seem strange at first, but the getthumb.php file contains all the information that the browser needs to display an image. However, if there are any errors in this file or in the thumbnail class file, the image will fail to display, and there will be no warning or error message, regardless of how you have configured your php.ini file. The error message will simply be interpreted as the binary output expected by the img tag.

NOTE   *In order to see error messages and warnings when debugging the ThumbnailImage class file, you need to call the getthumb.php file directly and not set it as the src for an img tag. Do this by hard-coding an image filename directly into the getthumb.php file and typing getthumb.php in the browser address bar.*

Where to Go from Here

Using the ThumbnailImage class enhances your ability to display a directory of images by reducing the size of the images. This is a definite improvement in both aesthetics and performance, because small images download faster and use up less screen real estate.

But what if the image directory contains a few hundred or even a few thousand images? Showing a large number of image files, even if they're only thumbnails, places unacceptable demands on server and client resources, and creates a web page that is far too long. You need to limit the number of images that display at any one time. Chapter 7 tackles this problem.

7

BUILDING THE
PAGENAVIGATOR CLASS

When there are a large number of images in a directory, it's not desirable to display all of them on one web page because doing so will probably create a very large and long page. Web pages should be of reasonable length and should not take too long to download. Rather than dumping all your images onto one page, use a page navigator to step through them in an orderly fashion. This chapter will take on the task of creating a navigator class; Chapter 8 will use this class in conjunction with the DirectoryItems class.

Before you can create a page navigator, you need to determine how it should behave. Keep its design flexible and make sure that its appearance is easily configurable so that it can blend with the style of any particular page.

How Will the Navigator Behave?

A good starting point is to look at the navigator at the bottom of a Google query page. When searching Google, the default settings show 10 results per page and the navigator appears across the bottom of the page. One navigates by clicking the Previous or Next links, by choosing a page number, or by clicking one of the many "o"s in Google. If your query returns a large number of pages, not all pages are shown in the page navigator. Records are ordered by relevance to the search criteria. Given this ordering scheme, there is little incentive to move to the last page of results and, in fact, there is no easy way of doing so.

Different Kinds of Searches

However, in many cases, searches return a relatively small number of items, and records are often ordered alphabetically. In situations such as this there should be an easy way to move to the beginning and the end pages, in addition to being able to move Previous and Next. Too, as with Google, the ability to configure the number of items shown per page is also desirable.

You should also limit the number of pages or links shown at any one time by your page navigator and make this option configurable to accommodate different needs and situations. For example, if you have 2,000 items to display and you're showing 10 items per page, it's probably not advisable to show all 200 links across the bottom of one page. But at the same time, you should show the total number of pages and identify the current page so that the user is not left in the dark.

Finally, the display style of navigation buttons should be configurable so that they match the design of an existing page. The best way to do this is to assign them a class name and manipulate their style using Cascading Style Sheets (CSS).

What Will It Look Like?

In sum, you will design a page navigator that will look something like Figure 7-1.

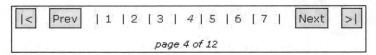

Figure 7-1: Your page navigator design

In this particular example, the maximum number of pages shown by your navigator is 7. The total number of pages is 12, and the link to the current page, 4, is disabled (indicated above by an italicized number). Each button and page number functions as a hyperlink (except for that of the current page). The button labeled |< displays the first page, and the button labeled >| displays the last page. In this particular example, the Next button displays page 5, and the Prev button displays page 3.

Now look at Figure 7-1 again, and note that pages 8 through 12 are not displayed. You can go directly to page 12 by clicking the >| button, but there is no way to go directly to pages 8 through 11. At what point should links to these pages become visible?

Apply this question to the Google navigator, and you'll see that the answer is not very straightforward. Among other things, it depends on the direction you want to move and the number of items your search returns.

In some situations, the number of page links shown doubles. You probably don't want to emulate this behavior, because your navigator will be used in a variety of situations, and in some cases space will be at a premium.

If you look more closely at a Google query, you can get a few hints about how to implement other desired behavior. For instance, try the following: Perform a Google query and put your mouse over one of the page number links in the navigator. If you look at the status bar of your browser, you see a query string that includes the variable start. If you haven't changed Google's default setting of 10 items per page, the value assigned to this variable is always a multiple of 10 that increases by 10 as the page numbers increase.

You'll use a similar technique in your page navigator. Your navigator will be a series of hyperlinks, each including a query string containing a page number indicating an offset from the start.

The Code

Go ahead and download the code for your page navigator, and look it over. Notice that there are considerably more data members than in other classes discussed so far. Names have been chosen in an attempt to make the purpose of the variable explicit, and related variables have been grouped. We'll discuss these variables in the order in which they appear in the class file.

```
private $pagename;
```

The variable $pagename is the name of the page that will contain the page navigator control. It could be replaced by $_SERVER['PHP_SELF'], but by using a variable, you can accommodate situations where the Apache module mod_rewrite is being used to rewrite URLs. It's designed to hold a string.

```
private $totalpages;
```

$totalpages is a convenient way to refer to the total number of pages required to display all the items in your list of images. It is calculated from the total number of items and the number of items shown per page. Its value will be an integer.

```
private $recordsperpage;
private $maxpagesshown;
```

$recordsperpage is the number of items shown on a page and $maxpagesshown is the maximum number of links to additional pages shown on any one page. The former affects the length of the page, while the latter affects the width of the navigator. Again, these are intended to be integer variables.

```
private $currentstartpage;
private $currentendpage;
private $currentpage;
```

$currentstartpage, $currentendpage, and $currentpage are best understood using a visual example. Refer back to Figure 7-1; these would be 1, 7, and 4, respectively.

The next four variables are string variables that hold the HTML code necessary to display inactive links.

```
//next and previous inactive
private $spannextinactive;
private $spanpreviousinactive;
//first and last inactive
private $firstinactivespan;
private $lastinactivespan;
```

If you are currently on the first page, moving to a previous page or to the first page itself wouldn't make sense. These variables will be used in place of active hyperlinks. Inactive links will be enclosed by span tags. Assigning a CSS class name to these spans allows their appearance to be manipulated by a style sheet.

$firstparamname and $params are data members that will form the query string in each hyperlink in your navigator.

```
//must match $_GET['offset'] in calling page
private $firstparamname = "offset";
//use as "&amp;name=value" pair for getting
private $params;
```

$firstparamname is assigned a default value of "offset." While the additional parameters contained in $params may or may not be added to the query string, the use of the "offset" parameter is not optional; this variable's name must always be matched by a $_GET['offset'] in the page that contains your navigator. The $firstparamname will perform the same function as start in a Google query string—you will always need to know where the current page is relative to the start page. The variable $params will hold any other name/value pairs that may be needed as part of a query string. (You'll learn more about this in Chapter 9.)

The next set of variables are string values that hold the CSS class names for the page navigator and its elements.

```
//css class names
private $divwrappername = "navigator";
private $pagedisplaydivname = "totalpagesdisplay";
private $inactivespanname = "inactive";
```

You've assigned default values to each of these variables, but they all have set and get methods so a client programmer can change them in order to match existing CSS classes if need be. $divwrappername is the name of the div tag that encloses the complete navigator. $pagedisplaydivname allows you to separately manipulate the display of the message relating the current page and total number of pages, such as *page 4 of 12.* You only need one class name for all of your inactive spans, because you want them all to have the same look.

The remaining four variables are simply text strings that label the controls used in the navigator, and they can be changed as the user sees fit:

```
//text for navigation
private $strfirst = "|&lt;";
private $strnext = "Next";
private $strprevious = "Prev";
private $strlast = "&gt;|";
//for error reporting
private $errorstring;
```

The use of variables for the navigation text means that a client programmer can configure these values—the look of the navigator is not fixed and can be adjusted to accommodate different visual layouts. The final data member is a string variable used for error reporting.

The Constructor

Now let's see how the class is constructed. The constructor accepts six arguments, two of which have default values. Here is the constructor declaration:

```
public function __construct($pagename, $totalrecords, $recordsperpage,
$recordoffset, $maxpagesshown = 4, $params = "")
```

Four of the parameters to the constructor are simply copied into their class equivalents, and all have been discussed in the previous section on the data members.

```
$this->pagename = $pagename;
$this->recordsperpage = $recordsperpage;
$this->maxpagesshown = $maxpagesshown;
//already urlencoded
$this->params = $params;
```

Note that $params (the variable that contains any additional parameters as a name/value pair) is not URL-encoded within the class. If it is used, it will need to be URL-encoded before it is sent.

The constructor finishes with calls to a number of private class methods:

```
//check recordoffset a multiple of recordsperpage
$this->checkRecordOffset($recordoffset, $recordsperpage) or
     die($this->errorstring);
$this->setTotalPages($totalrecords, $recordsperpage);
$this->calculateCurrentPage($recordoffset, $recordsperpage);
$this->createInactiveSpans();
$this->calculateCurrentStartPage();
$this->calculateCurrentEndPage();
```

Let's look at each of these method calls in turn.

Ain't Misbehavin'

If you want your navigator to behave properly, you can check some of the values passed to the constructor; that's exactly what the checkRecordOffset method does. It terminates construction of your object if it returns false. Let's see why.

```
private function checkRecordOffset($recordoffset, $recordsperpage){
    $bln = true;
    if($recordoffset%$recordsperpage != 0){
        $this->errorstring = "Error - not a multiple of records per page.";
        $bln = false;
    }
    return $bln;
}
```

The $recordoffset variable passed to the constructor tells the navigator where it is currently positioned.

Since you are paging through your list while keeping the number of items shown per page constant, the record offset must be a multiple of the number of items shown per page. If it's not, the navigator may still function but its behavior will be erratic. For this reason, the error message variable is set, a value of false is returned, and the application terminates. Terminating the application and identifying the reason saves having to debug a misbehaving application.

Other Constructor Method Calls

The five remaining private method calls made from the constructor aren't quite as interesting as the checkRecordOffset method, but a few comments are appropriate.

Determining the Total Number of Pages

Since your navigator always allows you to move to the last item, you need to know the total number of pages:

```
private function setTotalPages($totalrecords, $recordsperpage){
    $this->totalpages = ceil($totalrecords/$recordsperpage);
}
```

You use the ceil function to round up, because your final page may be a partial page.

For example, if you have 101 items to display, and you are showing 10 items per page, the first 10 pages will each show 10 items while the 11th page will show only one.

Determining the Current Page

In addition to the total number of pages, you also need to know the current page, so you have a calculateCurrentPage method:

```
private function calculateCurrentPage($recordoffset, $recordsperpage){
    $this->currentpage = $recordoffset/$recordsperpage;
}
```

Simply dividing the record offset by the records per page gives you the current page. Notice that if you're at the beginning of your list, the value of $recordoffset is 0, so the first page is also 0. This makes sense from a programming point of view, but before displaying the current page to a user, it's incremented by 1.

Inactive Spans

The following method—createInactiveSpans—prepares the HTML code necessary to display inactive Next, First, Previous, and Last links:

```
private function createInactiveSpans(){
  $this->spannextinactive = "<span class=\"".
    "$this->inactivespanname\">$this->strnext</span>\n";
  $this->lastinactivespan = "<span class=\"".
    "$this->inactivespanname\">$this->strlast</span>\n";
  $this->spanpreviousinactive = "<span class=\"".
    "$this->inactivespanname\">$this->strprevious</span>\n";
  $this->firstinactivespan = "<span class=\"".
    "$this->inactivespanname\">$this->strfirst</span>\n";
}
```

While setting these variables is not strictly necessary (there may, in fact, not be any inactive spans on a particular page), by creating a method to prepare inactive links beforehand, you unclutter your code and make the logic of the most important method—getNavigator—clearer.

Finding the Start Page

Since links to all pages are not always shown, page 1 is not always the first link on a page. For this reason you need to determine the current start page. For example, if the total number of items is 100 with 5 items per page, and you are showing 4 links in your navigator and the current page is 6, the current start page for the navigator will be 5.

```
private function calculateCurrentStartPage(){
    $temp = floor($this->currentpage/$this->maxpagesshown);
    $this->currentstartpage = $temp * $this->maxpagesshown;
}
```

Calculating the Current End Page

The last page displayed in the navigator is easily calculated once the first page has been determined:

```
private function calculateCurrentEndPage(){
    $this->currentendpage = $this->currentstartpage + $this->maxpagesshown;
    if($this->currentendpage > $this->totalpages){
      $this->currentendpage = $this->totalpages;
    }
}
```

The current end page is the current page plus the maximum number of pages shown, unless that number is greater than the total number of pages, in which case, the end page is equal to the total number of pages.

The getNavigator Method

We've covered the data members, the constructor, and some related private methods of the page navigator class, but it's the public methods that allow you to use it.

The get and set methods basically allow manipulation or retrieval of the CSS class names for the various components in the navigator, so we won't spend time on them. The method that performs most of the work in this class is the getNavigator method. It returns a string of the HTML-encoded links that make up your navigator. The navigator (shown in Figure 7-1) is created by starting at the left with the Move First link and finishes on the right with the Move Last link. We'll discuss the code piece by piece and relate it back to this figure. The declaration of this method is:

```
public function getNavigator()
```

The very first responsibility of this method is to wrap the entire navigator in a div tag and assign a class name to this div. Doing so allows you to manipulate the appearance of your navigator via CSS:

```
$strnavigator = "<div class=\"$this->divwrappername\">\n";
```

Move First and Move Previous

The first element displayed is the hyperlink that allows you to move to the very first page of items. It's disabled if the current page is the first page; if the current page is not the first page, you call a private class method—createLink—to create the hyperlink.

```
//output movefirst button
if($this->currentpage == 0){
    $strnavigator .= $this->firstinactivespan;
```

```
    }else{
        $strnavigator .= $this->createLink(0, $this->strfirst);
    }
```

The `createLink` method to create the hyperlink is as follows:

```
private function createLink($offset, $strdisplay ){
    $strtemp = "<a href=\"$this->pagename?$this->firstparamname=";
    $strtemp .= $offset;
    $strtemp .= "$this->params\">$strdisplay</a>\n";
    return $strtemp;
}
```

This method constructs a hyperlink that includes a query string containing the required offset parameter and any additional parameters that may be needed. For a Move First button, this link appears as l< if the default value of the variable—$strfirst—has not been altered.

The same logic applies to the Move Previous link, which is disabled if the current page is the first page:

```
//output moveprevious button
    if($this->currentpage == 0){
        $strnavigator .= $this->spanpreviousinactive;
    }else{
        $strnavigator .= $this->createLink($this->currentpage-1, $this-
>strprevious);
    }
```

Main Body of the Navigator

The main body of the navigator (see Listing 7-1) is created by looping through the pages, starting with the current start page.

```
    //loop through displayed pages from $currentstart
    ❶for($x = $this->currentstartpage; $x < ❷$this->currentendpage; $x++){
        //make current page inactive
        if($x == ❸$this->currentpage){
            $strnavigator .= "<span class=\"$this->inactivespanname\">";
            $strnavigator .= $x + 1;
            $strnavigator .= "</span>\n";
        }else{
            $strnavigator .= $this->createLink($x, $x+1);
        }
    }
```

Listing 7-1: The main body of the navigator

This ❶ for loop creates hyperlinks for all the pages except the current page, and the number of iterations is determined by ❷ the $currentendpage data member.

As with the Move First button, ❸ the current page will be inactive, but all other pages will be hyperlinks.

Move Next and Move Last

Finally, create the Move Next and Move Last buttons in the same manner as the Move First and the Move Previous buttons, as shown in Listing 7-2.

```
//next button
if($this->currentpage == $this->totalpages-1){
  $strnavigator .= $this->spannextinactive;
}else{
  $strnavigator .= $this->createLink($this->currentpage + 1, $this->strnext);
}
//move last button
if($this->currentpage == $this->totalpages-1){
  $strnavigator .= $this->lastinactivespan;
}else{
  $strnavigator .= $this->createLink($this->totalpages -1, $this->strlast);
}
```

Listing 7-2: Creating the Move Next and Move Last buttons

Current and Total Number of Pages

The navigator proper is complete, but information about the current page and the total number of pages helps orient the user:

```
$strnavigator .= ❶"</div>\n";
$strnavigator .= $this->getPageNumberDisplay();
return $strnavigator;
```

A terminating div tag (❶) encloses the navigator, and a call to getPageNumberDisplay creates the HTML code to display the current page and the total number of pages.

```
private function getPageNumberDisplay(){
    $str = "<div class=\"$this->pagedisplaydivname\">\nPage ";
    $str .= $this->currentpage + 1;
    $str .= " of $this->totalpages";
    $str .= "</div>\n";
    return $str;
}
```

NOTE   *The string that displays the current page and the total number of pages is enclosed within a separate div tag in order to easily manipulate its placement and appearance.*

Where to Go from Here

You've developed a page navigator class that implements behavior similar to the Google navigator. You've learned how to set the number of items shown per page and adjust the width of the navigator. The major components of the navigator have been assigned CSS class names, allowing manipulation of the navigator's appearance. Chapter 8 will demonstrate how to use the page navigator in conjunction with the DirectoryItems class and the ThumbnailImage class, and how to configure its appearance.

8

USING THE PAGENAVIGATOR CLASS

In this chapter we'll use the PageNavigator class to step through a directory of images reduced on the fly using the ThumbnailImage class. We'll use all three of the classes you have developed so far:

- The DirectoryItems class stores a list of filenames of images.
- The ThumbnailImage class reduces the dimensions of each image.
- The PageNavigator class steps through these images in an orderly fashion.

We'll also look at how to use CSS classes to adjust the appearance of the page navigator; this will greatly improve the reusability of the class. (This isn't directly related to object-oriented programming [OOP], but if a class's appearance cannot blend with various different designs, then its usefulness—and reusability—is greatly compromised. A web development language should integrate well with other web technologies.)

DirectoryItems Change

Fortunately, because the list of images in the `DirectoryItems` class is an array, you can use the ready-made PHP function to return a portion of an array—`array_slice`. All you need to do is wrap this function inside a method. Here is the additional method you require:

```
public function getFileArraySlice($start, $numberitems){
    return array_slice($this->filearray, $start, $numberitems);
}
```

The `$start` variable passed to this method performs the same function as the start variable in the Google query string discussed in Chapter 7. The `$numberitems` variable sets the number of items you wish to display per page. In a way, the entire `PageNavigator` class is an answer to the question, "How can you pass values to the `getArraySlice` method so that you can step through the list of images in an orderly fashion?"

CSS and Reusability

No matter how reusable an object is, it won't be reused if it can't be adapted to fit to a variety of page designs. Unlike the `DirectoryItems` class, which does its work on the server, the navigator *is* client-side HTML—it is a series of enabled or disabled hyperlinks. It's important to control the page navigator's appearance, because it's a component of a web page. Figure 8-1 shows that page navigator again.

Figure 8-1: The page navigator

Recall that in order to control the navigator's appearance, you wrapped it in a div tag and set the class attribute of the div tag to navigator. One way to display this component is to shrink the font by setting the `font-size` property to `smaller` and to use the `text-align` property to center the text. Here's how the CSS code to produce that effect might look:

```
div.navigator{
    font-size:smaller;
    padding:5px;
    text-align:center;
}
```

This CSS code will ensure that the navigator is centered and that the font size of its buttons is smaller than the surrounding text.

The div tag of the class, `totalpagesdisplay`, manipulates the appearance of the total page count in the following way:

```
div.totalpagesdisplay{
    ❶ font-style:italic;
    ❷ font-size:8pt;
    text-align:center;
    ❸ padding-top:15px;
}
```

A different ❶ font style and ❷ size are appropriate for displaying the current page and the total page count (*page 3 of 6*, as shown in Figure 8-1). Increased ❸ padding at the top separates the page number display from the navigator proper, which improves readability.

You'll make the anchor tags within your navigator distinctive by assigning style characteristics to them. Because the `inactive` spans will share some of those characteristics, you can define them here as well. Those shared properties might look something like the following:

```
.navigator a, span.inactive{
    margin-left:0px;
    border-top:1px solid ❶#999999;
    border-left:1px solid ❶#999999;
    border-right:1px solid ❷#000000;
    border-bottom:1px solid ❷#000000;
    padding: 0px 5px 2px 5px;
}
```

Using ❶ a lighter color for the top and left borders and then ❷ a darker color for the bottom and right borders outlines the links and creates the illusion of depth.

Assign properties to the anchor pseudo-classes in order to override the default behavior—they should be different from other anchors on this page:

```
.navigator ❶a:link, .navigator ❶a:visited,
        .navigator ❶a:hover,.navigator ❶a:active{
    color: #3300CC;
    background-color: #FAEBF7;
    text-decoration: none;
}
```

Because these hyperlinks look like buttons, it makes sense to assign the same characteristics to each of the different states represented by ❶ the pseudo-classes: link, visited, hover, and active.

Finally, you differentiate inactive links from active ones by changing the background and the font style. For example, in Figure 8-1, because page 3 is the current page, it is disabled and has a gray background and italic font style.

```
span.inactive{
    background-color :#EEEEEE;
    font-style:italic;
}
```

You can, of course, style your own navigator much differently, using different CSS styles and, really, that's the whole point.

Paging with Class

In Chapter 6, we created a web page to loop through a directory of images and display a thumbnail of each image. We're going to do the same thing here, but this time we'll incorporate the page navigator in order to display a limited number of images per page.

The very first thing you need to do is include the classes you'll be using. This is done with two require statements:

```
require 'PageNavigator.php';
require 'DirectoryItems.php';
```

The PERPAGE variable defines how many images to display on each page. Define it as a constant (5), because it is used in a number of different places on this page and you don't want to change its value accidentally:

```
//max per page
define("PERPAGE", 5);
```

Recall that within the PageNavigator, the variable called $firstparam is assigned a default value of offset—the name for the first name/value pair of the query string associated with the URL of each hyperlink in the navigator. Each page needs to retrieve the offset value in order to determine which group of images to display:

```
//name of first parameter in query string
define(❶"OFFSET", "offset");
/*get query string - name should be same as first parameter name
passed to the page navigator class*/
$offset = @$_GET[OFFSET];
```

Like PERPAGE, ❶ OFFSET is defined as a constant because you do not want its value to change. You want to ensure that the variable you're requesting matches the variable passed into this page by the navigator.

You also want the flexibility to open this page even when no query string has been passed. For this reason, you should check the value of $offset:

```
//check variable
if(!isset($offset)){
    ❶$totaloffset = 0;
```

```
    }
    else{
        //then calculate offset
        $totaloffset = $offset * ❷PERPAGE;
    }
```

If no query string is passed into the page, you want to begin displaying images at the beginning of your list, so you set ❶ $totaloffset to 0. If $offset does have a value, multiplying it by ❷ the PERPAGE value calculates the start position within the array of image filenames.

The name of the directory you want to use is assigned to the variable $directory:

```
$directory = "graphics";
$di = new DirectoryItems($directory);
```

Listing 8-1: Hard-coded directory name

Because you want to display the directory of images in the graphics directory, pass the value graphics to the constructor of the DirectoryItems class.

The imagesOnly method filters out all non-images, and the method naturalCaseInsensitiveOrder ignores case and orders numerically where appropriate.

```
$di->imagesOnly();
$di->naturalCaseInsensitiveOrder();
```

In Chapter 6, when you displayed all the thumbnails on one page, you retrieved the entire list of filenames from the DirectoryItems class instance. Since the page navigator controls the starting position and since you can retrieve a slice of the array, you need only retrieve a specific number of items here. Do this by passing the getArraySlice method a start position and the number of items you wish to display.

```
//get portion of array
$filearray = $di->getFileArraySlice($totaloffset, PERPAGE);
```

Displaying an Array Slice

You retrieve each filename and pass it to the getthumb.php file so it can serve as the file source for an img tag. You don't need to make any changes to the version of the getthumb.php file you used in Chapter 6—it includes the ThumbnailImage class and uses it to create a reduced image.

The code to loop through the thumbnail images hasn't changed from Chapter 6 either. For ease of reference, it's reproduced in Listing 8-2.

```
echo "<div style=\"text-align:center;\">";
echo "Click the file name to view full-sized version.<br />";
$path = "";
//specify size of thumbnail
$size = 100;
foreach (❶$filearray as $key => $value){
    $path = "$directory/".$key;
    /*errors in getthumb or in class will result in broken links
    - error will not display*/
    echo "<img src=\"getthumb.php?path=$path&amp;size=$size\" ".
    "style=\"border:1px solid black;margin-top:20px;\" ".
    "alt= \"$value\" /><br />\n";
    echo "<a href=\"$path\" target=\"_blank\" >";
    echo "Title: $value</a> <br />\n";
}
echo "</div><br />";
```

Listing 8-2: Code to loop through thumbnail images

This code differs from the code in Chapter 6 only in that ❶ the `$filearray` variable that contains the image filenames is the portion of the total array retrieved by the `getArraySlice` method and not all the filenames.

Creating the PageNavigator Object

In order to create the page navigator, you need the current page name and also the total number of image files; the global `$_SERVER` array supplies the name of the current page and `getCount` the total number of images.

```
$pagename = basename($_SERVER["PHP_SELF"]);
$totalcount = $di->getCount();
```

You only need to create the navigator if there is more than one page, so calculate that number first, as shown in the code in Listing 8-3.

```
$numpages = ceil($totalcount/PERPAGE);
//create if needed
if($numpages > 1){
    //create navigator
    $nav = new PageNavigator(❶$pagename, $totalcount, PERPAGE, $totaloffset);
    //is the default but make explicit
    ❷$nav->setFirstParamName(OFFSET);
    echo ❸$nav->getNavigator();
}
```

Listing 8-3: Creating the navigator if there's more than one page

When constructing the `PageNavigator` instance, you pass it ❶ the four required parameters and let the two additional parameters—`$maxpagesshown` and `$params`—default to 4 and an empty string, respectively. This means that the navigator will show links to a maximum of four pages and that there are no additional name/value pairs for the query string. (As promised in Chapter 7, you'll learn more about `$params` in Chapter 9. However, you may already have surmised that this variable can be used to replace the hard-coded directory name given in Listing 8-1.)

You do not need to set ❷ the first parameter name; it has a default value of `offset`. However, by setting the name here, you make it clear that this is the name of the one required name/value pair, and that it can be changed if desired.

Finally, the HTML code that makes up ❸ the navigator is returned and displayed in the web page.

Where to Go from Here

Using the `PageNavigator` class solves two problems: it alleviates the demand on server resources and it improves the aesthetics of the web page display. Only a limited number of images are displayed at any one time, thus reducing the demands on the server. Aesthetic requirements are satisfied by reduced web page length.

As noted on many occasions, the real value of objects is in their reusability. Through the use of CSS, you're able to adjust the appearance of the page navigator to match it to a variety of situations. By using `span` and `div` tags, you can manipulate the look and feel of the navigator so that it blends easily with any design. The number of items shown on each page and the number of pages accessible at any one time can be set to any number desired.

We've seen that the `PageNavigator` class's design is adaptable and that you can use it to step through an array of images, but what about its use in other situations? A navigator is much more commonly required with database queries that return a large number of records. In the next chapter, we'll develop a database class and then see how well the `PageNavigator` class can handle a large result set. The ability to reuse the navigator class in various and different circumstances will be a true test of its robustness.

9

DATABASE CLASSES

The last chapter ended by saying we would create a database class in order to test the versatility of the page navigator. That's what we're going to do in this chapter. I noted earlier that it's sometimes difficult to identify objects, because often what's needed is something conceptual rather than something physical and concrete. The database class or classes that we are going to create in this chapter are definitely of this nature. We can probably determine some of the requirements by looking at the DirectoryItems class—after all, as you learned in Chapter 5, this class is similar to a database table.

Using What You Know

Pursuing this line of thought, you need to:

- Filter and order records
- Know the total number of records
- Be able to extract sequential subsets of the total

In the context of database classes, the description of the requirements immediately suggests the use of the SQL ORDER BY, WHERE, and LIMIT clauses to order, filter, and extract subsets respectively. You had to create this kind of functionality for the DirectoryItems class, but why recreate what's already available in SQL?

Just as PHP's built-in image manipulation functions helped create the ThumbnailImage class, look also for assistance from the existing MySQL-related functions. If you've used these functions before, you'll immediately know which ones are the most important and the most commonly required. Obviously, you'll need mysql_connect to create a connection to a specific server. Creating a connection is a prerequisite for using mysql_select_db to select a database and mysql_query to execute a query and return a result set of rows.

One Lump or Two?

There are two distinct classes that can be built around these existing PHP MySQL functions, depending upon your preferences: a connection class and a result set class. First, you'll create a database connection class, as you might imagine, making use of the mysql_connect function. A connection is server-specific and can be used to create any number of result sets taken from any database on that server. It simply sets up communication between a web page and a database server. A result set makes use of a connection in order to update or display data. You'll build a MySQL result set class around the mysql_select_db and mysql_query functions.

You will develop fairly skeletal versions of these two classes, emphasizing any unexplored areas of object-oriented programming (OOP). Nevertheless, these classes will be perfectly fit for the task of testing the versatility of the PageNavigator class.

In this chapter, we'll take a slightly different approach to the code. I'll show the data members and the methods of the class, but I'll only reproduce code that requires comment. As usual, the complete code is available at the companion website, so don't hesitate to download it and refer to it if you find this helpful.

The MySQLConnect Class

The MySQLConnect class is a fairly modest class with only two data members and four public methods.

```
//data members
private $connection
private static $instances = 0
//methods
public function __construct($hostname, $username, $password)
public function __destruct()
public function createResultSet($strSQL, $databasename)
public function close()
```

What is immediately noteworthy about this class is the use of the keyword static to modify a data member. Identifying a variable as static means that it is shared among all instances of a class. If one instance changes the value of a static variable, it is changed for all instances. Unique variables are created each time a class is instantiated, and they belong to that specific instance. Not so with static variables—they belong to the class as a whole (and for this reason are sometimes referred to as *class variables*). Let's look at the code for the constructor and see how this can be useful.

A Class-Conscious Variable

The parameters passed to the constructor are those necessary to make a database connection using the built-in PHP function, mysql_connect. Again, this method is a wrapper method but with a few additional bells and whistles.

```
public function __construct($hostname, $username, $password){
    if(❶MySQLConnect::$instances == 0){
        $this->connection = mysql_connect($hostname,$username,$password) or
        die ( mysql_error(). " Error no:".mysql_errno());
        MySQLConnect::$instances = 1;
    }else{
        $msg = "Close the existing instance of the ".
        "MySQLConnect class.";
        die($msg);
    }
}
```

This class won't be instantiated if there is already an existing instance. If the $instances variable has a value of 0, a connection is made to the server, and the value of $instances is set to 1. Checking the value of this static variable makes sense because it is shared among all instances, it's available to all instances, and its value is the same for all instances.

The syntax for referencing a static variable (❶) is different from that used to reference a normal data member. It would not make sense to use the pseudo-variable $this with $instances, since $this refers to the current object and by definition, static variables belong to the class rather than a specific instance. Quite sensibly, the class name is used instead, and the arrow operator is replaced by a double colon—the scope resolution operator.

The *scope resolution operator* is principally used when referencing static data members or static methods. In Chapter 10 you'll see the two other occasions when this operator is used, but for now you need only concern yourself with its use with static data members. When referencing a static variable from within its class, you also have the option of replacing the class name with the keyword self. In this case, the expression self::$instances is equivalent to MySQLConnect::$instances. Static members referenced outside the confines of their class must use the class name. You don't need to worry about that here, since $instances is private and cannot be referenced outside the MySQLConnect class.

At this point you may be thinking, "That's all well and good, but why would I want a class that I can only create one instance of?" Creating a database connection is an expensive operation so restricting creation of connections conserves resources.

NOTE   *By restricting the connection class to a single instance, we are mimicking the built-in* `mysql_connect` *function. Its default behavior is to reuse a connection resource rather than create a new one.*

However, there are some circumstances where a new connection is a necessity.

Making Other Connections

Two different connection objects are required if a single script needs to connect to two different servers. The `close` method makes it possible to connect to a different server.

```
public function close(){
    MySQLConnect::$instances = 0;
    if(isset($this->connection)){
        mysql_close($this->connection);
        unset($this->connection);
    }
}
```

Two instances of the `MySQLConnect` class can exist, but not simultaneously. If you want to create a connection to another server, you must first close the existing connection. The `close` method closes the current connection and resets the static variable `$instances` to 0. Manipulating the `$instances` variable in this way allows you to create a new connection, but only after the current one is closed.

Explicitly closing a connection and unsetting it makes for clearer error messages should you accidentally call a result set method after closing its connection. The requirement to close the current connection also serves as a reminder that a result set is a dependent object.

To make this even clearer, let's look at how a result set is created.

You Can Only Get There from Here

The following method serves as a very strong reminder that you first need a connection in order to create a result set:

```
public function createResultSet($strSQL, $databasename){
    $rs = new MySQLResultSet($strSQL, $databasename, $this->connection );
    return $rs;
}
```

The creation of a `MySQLResultSet` requires a reference to the `connection` data member of the `MySQLConnect` class. This data member is private and does not have an accessor method, so it's only available from within the `MySQLConnect` class. Short of reverting to procedural programming to create a connection resource, you cannot create an instance of the MySQLResultSet class except by using this method of the MySQLConnect class. This makes it very clear that a result set is a dependent object. You can't create one without first having a connection to a server. Instantiating an object of the MySQLResultSet class from within the MySQLConnect class serves not only to remind you of this dependency, but it enforces it programmatically. To understand the connection class, you've had to look ahead at the constructor for the result set class.

Let's examine the rest of this class in detail.

The MySQLResultSet Class

Not surprisingly, the MySQLResultSet class (shown in Listing 9-1) has more data members and methods than the MySQLConnect class. However, in many ways, it's a much simpler class and requires much less explanation. To get an overview of this class, find all its data members and methods listed here:

```
//data members
private $strSQL
private $databasename
private $connection
private $result
// public methods
public function __construct($strSQL, $databasename, $connection)
public function __destruct()
//return current record
public function getRow()
//accessor method for returning database name
public function getDatabaseName()
public function getNumberColumns()
public function getNumberRows()
//get id of most recently inserted record
public function getInsertId()
//find total number without a LIMIT clause
public function getUnlimitedNumberRows()
public function getFieldNames()
public function findVersionNumber()
//private methods
//make sure the sql is a SELECT
private function checkForSelect()
//close result set and unset
private function close()
//version specific count methods
private function countVersionFour()
private function countVersionThree($tempsql, $end)
```

Listing 9-1: The MySQLResultSet class

You've already seen the constructor for this class, but a few general comments are in order before looking at any of the methods in more detail. One notable absence from the list of methods is a method equivalent to the getArraySlice method of the DirectoryItems class. You could have created something equivalent by selecting all the required records and then using the built-in function mysql_data_seek to reposition the record pointer as necessary, but the price to pay for this relatively easy implementation would be poor performance. Imagine paging through 1,000 records 10 records at a time and for each page, bringing over all 1,000 records. The more scalable solution is to restrict the number of records selected by using a LIMIT clause in the SQL that creates the result set.

However, in order for your page navigator to function, you also need to know the total number of records without a LIMIT clause. With MySQL versions 4.0 and higher, there is an easy way of doing this using SQL_CALC_FOUND_ROWS, followed by a call to the FOUND_ROWS function. For MySQL version 3, you can use the COUNT function without a LIMIT clause.

This is a fairly easy process to automate, so to make things easier on yourselves and your client programmers, you create the getUnlimitedNumberRows method. Briefly, the getUnlimitedNumberRows method confirms that the query is a SELECT, determines the MySQL version number, and discovers the total number of records that would be returned without a LIMIT clause by calling the private method countVersionThree or countVersionFour.

Most of the remaining methods are simply wrapper methods for existing MySQL functions, or they make use of these functions to perform fairly straightforward tasks. You won't actually be using some of these methods—getNumberColumns, for instance—but they give you an idea of how this class could be expanded.

This isn't the last you'll see of the MySQLResultSet class. We'll return to it again in Chapter 10 because it provides an ideal opportunity for further exploring OO programming. Right now though, your primary concern is to see how it functions with the PageNavigator class.

Using the Page Navigator

In order to use the page navigator to page through a result set, you'll need a database and a table. Almost any database will do; feel free to use one that you have at hand, but for your convenience, the following SQL statement creates the table used with the code example:

```
CREATE TABLE `tblbooks` (
  `inventorynumber` int(11) NOT NULL auto_increment,
  `cat` char(3) NOT NULL default '',
  `title` varchar(150) NOT NULL default '',
  `author` varchar(100) NOT NULL default '',
  `publisher` varchar(4) NOT NULL default '',
  `sold` tinyint(1) default 0,
  PRIMARY KEY  (`inventorynumber`),
  KEY `authidx` (`author`)
)
```

This is a fairly simple table, but it's perfectly adequate for your needs—as long as it's populated with a sufficient number of records. The example shows five records per page, so at least six records are required.

NOTE *The SQL to create this table and insert a number of records is available with the downloads for this chapter. Find the file* books.sql.

The code to use the page navigator with a result set is very similar to the code you used when testing the DirectoryItems class. I'll comment on the differences only.

```
require 'MySQLConnect.php';
require 'PageNavigator.php';
define("OFFSET", "offset");
//get query string
$offset = @$_GET[OFFSET];
//max per page
define("PERPAGE", 5);
//check variable
if (!isset($offset)){
    $recordoffset = 0;
}else{
    //calc record offset
    $recordoffset = $offset * PERPAGE;
}
```

To this point, the code is identical to the code in Chapter 8, but the MySQLConnect class replaces the DirectoryItems class. Remember that the MySQLResultSet class has been included within the MySQLConnect.php file, so it doesn't need to be included here with a require statement.

```
$category = ❶@$_GET["category"];
//check variable
if (!isset($category)){
    $category = "LIT";
}
```

To demonstrate the versatility of the PageNavigator class, another name/value pair is passed to this page. In addition to the $offset value, you pass in ❶ a $category value. Doing this allows you to use the identical query for any category of books you choose by simply adding another criterion to the WHERE clause of your SQL. Using the $category value also demonstrates, as I promised earlier, how the final parameter passed to the page navigator (in this case, $otherparameter) is used—but more about that shortly.

Ordering, Filtering, and Extracting

In plain English, your SQL statement (Listing 9-2) allows you to select the author and title for unsold books in the specified category. The books are ordered by the author name.

```
$strsql = "SELECT author, title ".
    "FROM tblbooks ".
    "WHERE sold = 0 AND cat = '$category' ".
    "ORDER BY author LIMIT ❶$recordoffset,". ❷PERPAGE;
```

Listing 9-2: The SQL statement

The `MySQLResultSet` class is created using a fairly simple SQL query with a `LIMIT` clause. This clause performs the same function as the `getArraySlice` method of the `DirectoryItems` class by selecting only a portion of the total. Notice that ❶ the first parameter—`$recordoffset`—indicates the start position within the result set, and ❷ the second parameter—`PERPAGE`—indicates the number of records that will be returned.

You create an instance of a `MySQLConnect` object by passing in the required parameters: host, username, and password.

```
$con = new MySQLConnect('localhost', 'webuser', 'webpassword');
```

For the sake of clarity, literal values are shown, but in a real-life situation, you would probably want to use variables rather than literals and perhaps for security reasons, locate the file that contains these variables outside the web directory. Substitute values appropriate to your MySQL database for the literals given above. Likewise with the database name used when creating a result set.

Using a method of the `MySQLConnect` object, you create a `MySQLResultSet`—`$rs`.

```
//get result set
$rs = $con->createResultSet($strsql, 'mydatabase');
```

The constructor for the result set class selects the database and executes the query against it.

Traversing the Result Set

All that remains before displaying your page navigator is to traverse the result and output it.

```
echo "<div style=\"text-align:center\">";
while($row = $rs->getRow()){
    echo $row[0]." - ".$row[1];
    echo "<br />\n";
}
echo "<br />";
echo "</div>\n";
```

The getRow method of a `MySQLResultSet` calls the PHP function `mysql_fetch_array`, retrieving the current record and moving the record pointer forward to the next record. (This is a perfectly adequate way of iterating through your results, but you will develop a different approach in Chapter 10.) There are only two fields in your result set, and both of these are echoed to the screen centered within a div tag.

Your Navigator Needs Directions

Next, you need to collect the information needed by the page navigator.

```
$pagename = basename($_SERVER['PHP_SELF']);
//find total number of records
$totalrecords = $rs->getUnlimitedNumberRows();
$numpages = ceil($totalrecords/PERPAGE);
```

In Chapter 8, the DirectoryItems class simply called the built-in count function of an array to determine the total number of items but here the method getUnlimitedNumberRows is used. This method returns the total number of records that there would be if the SQL statement shown in Listing 9-2 was executed without a LIMIT clause. Remember, the LIMIT clause allows you to return a selection of records much like the getFileArraySlice method of the DirectoryItems class.

```
//create category parameter
$otherparameters = "&amp;category=LIT";
```

It is often the case that web pages are invoked passing a query string that contains a number of name/value pairs; this is the purpose of the $otherparameters variable. When you used the PageNavigator class with the DirectoryItems class, you ignored this parameter and let it default to an empty string. Here, you are only passing one name/value pair, but any number may be passed as long as they are formatted properly using the character entity for an ampersand (&) and an equal sign (=). (In some cases, you may also need to URL-encode them.)

```
//create if needed
if($numpages > 1){
    //create navigator
    $nav = new PageNavigator($pagename, $totalrecords, PERPAGE,
        $recordoffset, 4, $otherparameters);
    echo $nav->getNavigator();
}
```

This PageNavigator instance is slightly different from the one in Chapter 8. In that chapter, you let the last two parameters default, but because you are making use of $otherparameters, and because this variable is the last value passed to the PageNavigator constructor, you have no choice but to specify all preceding values.

NOTE   *Remember that no parameter may have a default value if it is followed by a parameter with a specified value. (PHP enforces this at call time, not when the method is defined.)*

Recall that the second-to-last value passed to the navigator determines the width of the navigator and the number of links shown. In the preceding code, its value is 4.

How the navigator actually appears depends on the number of records in the `tblbooks` table and, of course, on how you have configured the CSS classes that control the navigator's appearance. If you have been following along and coding as you read, you'll see that the `PageNavigator` class functions every bit as well with a database as it did with the `DirectoryItems` class—it is a reusable object.

Where to Go After the Navigator

We developed these database classes because they are useful in themselves, but they also show the versatility of the `PageNavigator` class—this is not a one trick pony but a class that can be reused in a variety of situations. Along the way, you've also learned more about OOP and the process of class creation. This is not something that takes place in a vacuum. Knowledge of existing PHP functions and of SQL was essential to the process and conditioned the result. What you already know about PHP as a procedural programmer and about SQL has proven to be an invaluable asset.

In the next chapter we'll improve on the database classes introduced here and explore one of the most important concepts of OOP, inheritance. We'll also look at one of the classes built in to PHP 5, namely `Exception`. From now on we will make use of classes built in to PHP 5 so code compatible with PHP 4 can no longer be provided.

10

IMPROVEMENT THROUGH INHERITANCE

Anyone who has played Monopoly knows that a player's financial situation can be improved through inheritance. In object-oriented programming (OOP), inheritance can also bring improvement. In this chapter we'll use inheritance to improve the MySQL classes developed in Chapter 9, by simplifying error trapping and by modifying the behavior of the MySQLResultSet class.

Trapping errors is not a job that developers approach with enthusiasm. It is tedious and a distraction from the task at hand. No one sets out to write error-handling code; it is a necessary evil. Not only that, error trapping is ugly. It clutters up well-written code and often ends up obscuring what was initially readable. Further, it's not a good idea to write error trapping in the early stages of development because you want errors to be readily apparent. For these reasons error trapping is often left until the final stages of development and, if it is done at all, it is tacked on more or less as an afterthought.

One of the big advantages of OOP is the ability to catch exceptions rather than trap errors. By catching exceptions, the task of handling errors can be centralized. This makes for much tidier code and eases the transition from development to production code—erasing the need to tack on error trapping at the end.

This improvement to error handling is made possible because of a built-in class, Exception. In this chapter you will use this class as the base class for building your own exception class.

The second improvement we'll apply involves modifications to the user-defined class, MySQLResultSet. As you saw in the previous chapter, result sets and arrays have characteristics in common; you often need to iterate through them to examine each element. It is exceptionally easy to traverse an array by using a foreach loop. This easy traversal is the modification in behavior that we have in mind for the MySQLResultSet class. In this case, a built-in interface (rather than a class) facilitates adding this behavior to the MySQLResultSet class.

The Standard PHP Library

These planned improvements to the MySQL classes use the Standard PHP Library (SPL), a collection of classes and interfaces aimed at solving common programming problems. The SPL, new to PHP 5, is roughly comparable to the Standard Template Library in C++ or the many classes built in to the Java language. But whereas there are thousands of classes to draw upon in Java, the number available in PHP is much more modest.

We'll use the Exception class to form the basis for a MySQLException class and the SPL to adapt the MySQLResultSet class for use with a foreach loop by using the Iterator interface. Besides the classes belonging to the SPL, there are well over 100 built-in classes in PHP 5. We'll deal with some of the other built-in classes in Chapters 12, 14, 15, and 16.

Extending a Class Through Inheritance

One of the major advantages of OOP is that you don't always have to start from scratch. Existing classes may be able to do the job for you. If an existing class does exactly what's required, then you can simply use it "as is." If it does something similar, but not exactly what you need, you can adapt it. This process of adaptation is called *inheritance*.

Inheritance is one of the most important features of object-oriented (OO) languages. It allows us to create new classes from existing ones, exploiting behavior that is already defined and adjusting it as necessary. The term "inheritance" is appropriate because the data members and methods of the original class become part of the newly created class. However, as with genetic inheritance, the child may be similar to the parent in some respects but different in others.

Because a child class is derived from a parent class, it is also referred to as a *derived class*, and its parent is called the *base class*. Parent classes are also sometimes referred to as *superclasses* and derived classes as *subclasses*.

The Exception Class

The first step in inheriting from a class is to understand the structure of the parent class. For example, Listing 10-1 lists all the data members and methods of the Exception class.

```
protected $message;
protected $code;
protected $file;
protected $line;
private $string;
private $trace;
public function __construct($message = null, $code = 0);
public function __toString();
final public function getCode();
final public function getMessage();
final public function getFile();
final public function getLine();
final public function getTrace();
final public function getTraceAsString();
final private __clone();
```

Listing 10-1: Data members and methods of the Exception class

You'll notice some unfamiliar keywords (such as protected and final) as well as a couple of unfamiliar methods that begin with a double underscore (magic methods). We'll discuss each of these in turn.

protected

You should now have a good understanding of the keywords private and public as applied to data members or methods (if not, see Chapter 4). However, one additional piece of information about access modifiers not mentioned so far is that private methods or data members are not inherited by a derived class.

In some cases though, you may want new classes to inherit private data members. To do this, you use the access modifier, protected, in place of private. A *protected* data member, like a private data member, cannot be directly accessed outside its class, but it can be inherited and directly accessed by a derived class. In the specific case in question, any class derived from Exception will have direct access to $message, $code, $file, and $line, but no direct access to $string or $trace. This means that the following assignment is allowed from within a class derived from Exception:

```
$this->message = 'New Error';
```

and this is disallowed:

```
$this->string = 'Any string';
```

In addition to restricting access and controlling the way that a client programmer can use a class, the keywords private, protected, and public play a role in inheritance. Protected methods and data members are inherited by a derived class, but restricted access is preserved.

final

The keyword final also has meaning only in the context of inheritance.

When a method is defined as final, no derived class can change it. With non-final methods, a derived class can always redeclare the function and have it do something different. A class derived from the Exception class cannot create a new getCode method. On the other hand, there are no restrictions on creating a derived method called __toString.

NOTE *From the point of view of the class originator, the keyword final is a way of ensuring that certain elements of a class are not changed. Additionally, when final is applied to a class as a whole, nothing in that class can be changed.*

More Magic Methods

The Exception class contains two new magic methods. We'll discuss each in turn.

__toString

If the __toString method of a class is defined, it is invoked automatically whenever that class is displayed. For example, suppose you create an instance of the Exception class and want to echo it to the screen like so:

```
$e = new Exception();
echo $e;
```

The expected result when echoing a simple variable to the screen is obvious. For example, if the variable is an integer with the value of 5, you expect 5 to appear on the screen. However, if you echo an instance variable to the screen, and the __toString method is not defined, you'll see something like *Object id#3*. Because objects are composite, that is, they are made up of a number of data members and methods, it is not readily apparent what the string representation of an object should be.

The __toString method was introduced to control what happens when a class is displayed. It allows you to define a more meaningful string representation of your class. It is called "magic" because it is invoked in the background whenever an instance variable is the object of the print or echo functions. In the example code snippet above, when $e is output to the screen, an implicit call is made to the __toString method.

A __toString method can be a convenient way of looking at the properties of an object in much the same way that the print_r function displays all the keys and values of an array. (We'll examine this method again later in this chapter when we discuss the MySQLException class in connection with catching exceptions.)

__clone

The __clone method is a bit more problematic than __toString. Whereas __toString allows you to adjust the behavior of an object when it is displayed, __clone is invoked when you copy your object using the clone operator. This operator (new to PHP 5) allows you to create a copy of an object rather than just a reference to it. (For those of you familiar with other OO languages, this magic method acts like a copy constructor.)

You should generally implement the __clone method for any class that is an aggregate object. An aggregate object is an object that has at least one data member that is itself an object. For example, if both Player and Team are objects and Team contains Players, then Team is an aggregate object.

NOTE *See Chapter 13 for a more detailed description of the __clone method and the clone operator and for a more extensive treatment of aggregate classes.*

Replacing Errors with Exceptions

Before you create your derived class, let's look at the code that the MySQLException class will replace. The MySQLConnect class constructor provides a good example of how your exception class will be used.

Recall that your main goal when creating your own exception class is to rid your code of messy error trapping procedures. You've achieved this to some extent simply by incorporating error trapping into class methods, but you can reap further benefits.

In Listing 10-2, exceptions will replace the code that currently calls the die function. In the first case you ❶ terminate the program because mysql_connect cannot create a connection, whether because of an incorrect host, username, or password, or perhaps because the MySQL server is down. In any case, a look at the built-in error messages will help identify the problem and whether or not it is within your control.

```
function __construct($hostname, $username, $password){
    if(MySQLConnect::$instances == 0){
        $this->connection = mysql_connect($hostname, $username, $password) or
        ❶die(mysql_error(). " Error no: ".mysql_errno());
        MySQLConnect::$instances = 0;
    }else{
        $msg = "Close the existing instance of the ".
            "MySQLConnect class.";
        ❷die($msg);
    }
}
```

Listing 10-2: Code of MySQLConnect class constructor that calls the die function

In the second case ❷ execution is deliberately terminated because your class is being misused. You don't want a client programmer to attempt to open two connections simultaneously because one is all that's required. Here, you have two different kinds of errors, one of indeterminate cause and the other an instance of class misuse.

NOTE *Recall that because PHP is not a compiled language there is no such thing as a compile-time error. By creating your own exception class you partially remedy this situation by creating messages that indicate class misuse.*

The MySQLException Class

You can improve the functionality of a class when using inheritance by adding new methods or changing inherited ones. Changing inherited methods of a class is called *overriding*. In this particular case, the number of changes you can make to existing methods by overriding them is severely limited because, as you saw in Listing 10-1, there are only two non-final methods of the Exception class: the constructor and the __toString method. Let's change both of these methods (see Listing 10-3).

```
class MySQLException ❶extends Exception{
    //no new data members
    public function __construct($message, $errorno){
        //check for programmer error
        if($errorno >= 5000){
            $message = __CLASS__ ." type. Improper class usage. ". $message;
        }else{
            $message = __CLASS__ . " - ". $message;
        }
        //call the Exception constructor
        parent::__construct($message, $errorno);
    }
    //override __toString
    public function __toString(){
        return ("Error: $this->code - $this->message");
    }
}
```

Listing 10-3: Code to create the MySQLException class

To inherit from an existing class and add its functionality to a newly created class, use ❶ the keyword extends and the parent class name. Since Exception is a built-in class, there's no need to explicitly include any files. The keyword extends is all that's needed in order to give our newly created class immediate access to all the public and protected methods and data members of its parent. This is a very succinct and elegant way of reusing code.

Overridden Methods

Listing 10-3 shows all the code required to create a class derived from Exception. There are only two methods and both are overridden parent class methods.

But let's take a more detailed look, beginning with the constructor. Note how it checks the value of the error number. This test is designed to separate errors attributable to the programmer from all other errors.

We've chosen the range 5,000 and greater because this range is not used by built-in MySQL errors. The message associated with programmer errors indicates misuse of the class, and differentiating client programmer errors from other errors makes it easier to use the database classes.

For clarity, the error message includes the class name, which we avoid hard-coding by using the constant __CLASS__. After identifying the type of error, the Exception class constructor is called using the scope resolution operator and the keyword parent. (You encountered similar syntax when you referenced a static variable in Chapter 9.) This is the syntax for calling any parent method from within a derived class, and one of the few cases where it's necessary to invoke a magic method directly.

As you can see, there is no need to hard-code the parent class name because all constructors are invoked by calling __construct—the very reason for introducing a magic construction method in PHP 5.

NOTE *If a derived class overrides a parent constructor, there is no implicit call to the parent. The call must be made explicitly, as in Listing 10-3.*

The __toString method defined in Listing 10-3 replaces the __toString method inherited from the parent class. As a result, a MySQLException echoed to the screen shows only the error number and the associated message, which is much less informative than the __toString method of the parent class (which traces the error and shows its line number). This makes for more secure production code because it reduces the information associated with an exception, but it also makes development of applications more difficult. (You may want to comment out this code while debugging an application. By so doing, you revert to the more informative method of the parent.)

Changes to the MySQLConnect Class

The changes required so that the MySQLConnect class can use MySQLException objects are minimal. Of course the MySQLConnect class needs to know about this derived exception class, but this is easily accomplished with the following statement:

```
require 'MySQLException.php';
```

Next, you need an error code number that is greater than or equal to 5,000 (that is, outside the range used by MySQL). Then define a constant class value using the keyword const and give this constant a name using uppercase letters (per convention). The const keyword performs the same task for OOP as the define function does for procedural programming—it declares a variable that cannot be changed. Constant data members do not use access modifiers, so they are effectively public.

```
const ONLY_ONE_INSTANCE_ALLOWED = 5000;
```

The only other changes involve the constructor, as shown in Listing 10-4.

```
public function __construct($hostname, $username, $password){
    if(MySQLConnect::$instances == 0){
        if(!$this->connection = mysql_connect($hostname, $username,$password )){
          ❶throw new MySQLException(mysql_error(), ❷mysql_errno());
        }
        MySQLConnect::$instances = 1;
    }else{
        $msg = "Close the existing instance of the ".
          "MySQLConnect class.";
        throw new MySQLException(❸$msg, self::ONLY_ONE_INSTANCE_ALLOWED);
    }
}
```

Listing 10-4: Changes to the MySQLConnect constructor

Compare Listing 10-4 with Listing 10-2. Notice that the calls to the die function have been removed, and an exception has been constructed in their place. The new keyword throw (❶) is used exclusively with exceptions. It hands off the exception to be dealt with elsewhere (as you'll see in the following section).

The first MySQLException is constructed using ❷ the built-in MySQL error number and message. In the second case ❸ an appropriate message is created and the class constant, ONLY_ONE_INSTANCE_ALLOWED, is passed to the constructor. (Notice the syntax for referencing a class constant using the scope resolution operator and the keyword self; this is exactly the same way that a static variable is referenced.)

Prodding Your Class into Action

If you force an exception by attempting to create a second connection without closing the first one, you see this message:

```
Error: 5000 - MySQLException type. Improper class usage. Close the existing
instance of the MySQLConnect class.
```

This tells you the class the exception belongs to, that the error results from misuse of the class, and how to rectify the error.

Changes to the MySQLResultSet class are identical to the changes shown above. Constant data members with values greater than 5,000 are added to the class in order to identify class usage errors, but otherwise existing error numbers and messages are used. (We won't deal with the details here; to view those changes, download the files associated with this chapter.)

Catching Exceptions

You have now finished all the changes in your database classes that relate to exceptions. All you need to do now is to see how exceptions are caught by enclosing your code within a try block.

A *try block* is a programming structure that is used to enclose code that may cause errors. It is always followed by a catch block. An error, or more properly speaking an exception, that occurs within the try is thrown and handled by the catch. This is why a try/catch block is said to *handle* exceptions.

However, there are important differences between error trapping and exception handling. The argument to a catch clause is always an object. Any Exception that occurs within the scope of the try block will look for a catch that has a matching Exception type as its argument.

NOTE *The identification of the object type in a catch block is called* type hinting. *We'll discuss this in greater detail in Chapter 11.*

You should begin the try block immediately before the first line of code that might throw an exception (namely, where we create a connection object). Then enclose every subsequent line of code within the try block, except for the catch blocks. The code is otherwise identical to that in the page.php file, included with the file downloads for Chapter 9; only the relevant parts are reproduced in Listing 10-5.

```
try{
    $con = new MySQLConnect($hostname, $username, $password);
    //all remaining code
    ...
}
catch(MySQLException $e){
    echo $e;
    exit();
}
catch(Exception $e){
    echo $e;
    exit();
}
```

Listing 10-5: The try block and catch blocks, showing how exceptions are caught

You follow the try block with two catch blocks: one to catch the MySQLException class and the other to catch the parent class, Exception. Any code that throws an exception will be caught by one of the catch blocks.

A thrown exception looks for the first matching exception type in the following catch blocks. When it finds a match, it executes the code within that block. It ignores all other catch blocks (unless it is re-thrown). For example, if a MySQLException is thrown in the try block of Listing 10-5, it will be caught by the first catch, and the code in the second catch won't execute.

The order of the catch blocks is the inverse order of inheritance: The child class must precede its parent. Should the catch block for a parent class precede the child class, the exception will always be caught by the parent, and the child catch will be unreachable.

When using typical procedural error handling, you must check for errors immediately following the code that may cause problems. As you can see in Listing 10-5, an Exception may be caught many lines away from where the problem occurs, which is an advantage because it makes for more readable and maintainable code.

DEALING WITH EXCEPTIONS

Your catch blocks in Listing 10-5 simply output the error number and message and end the application; there's no need to recover from these exceptions or take any other action. But this isn't always the case. For example, suppose you create an application that allows users to create their own SQL statements to query a database. When errors in syntax occur it would make sense to display the error message and reload the web page rather than simply exit the application. There are some notable differences between error handling in PHP and other languages. For instance, PHP doesn't require that exceptions to be caught and does not support a finally block.

Implementing an Interface

Inheriting from an existing class is a very powerful tool in the OO programmer's arsenal. However, it's not always the appropriate one to use, because PHP doesn't allow a class to have more than one parent class.

This generally seems to be a good thing; it avoids the complexity that can be introduced with multiple inheritance. However, suppose that you had created a more abstract database result set class and derived your MySQLResultSet from it. With single inheritance it would be impossible for your class to also inherit from any other class.

For this reason PHP allows multiple inheritance, but only for interfaces. As you saw in Chapter 2, an *interface* is a class with no data members that declares but does not define methods (something that is left to the derived class). An interface acts like a skeleton, and the implementing class provides the body. Although a class can have only one parent class, it can implement any number of interfaces.

Listing 10-6 shows the code for the interface we wish to use to improve the MySQLResultSet class: the Iterator.

```
interface Iterator{
    public function current();
    public function key();
    public function next();
    public function rewind();
    public function valid();
}
```

Listing 10-6: Methods of the Iterator interface

Note that instead of beginning with the keyword class, Iterator begins with interface, but otherwise it looks like a class. Notice too that method names have access modifiers and that the method declarations are followed by semicolons. There are no braces following the method names because there is no implementation—which is precisely what makes an interface an interface. The interface is a skeleton; an implementing class must flesh it out.

Learning About the Iterator Interface

Here's a brief description of each method in the Iterator interface:

current	Returns the current element
key	Returns the key of the current element
next	Moves forward to the next element
rewind	Rewinds the iterator to the first element
valid	Checks to see if there is a current element after calls to rewind or next

A bit more can be gleaned from watching an iterator in action. For example, the code shown in Listing 10-7 traverses an iterable object using all of the methods in the Iterator interface.

```
$iterator->rewind();
while($iterator->valid()){
    echo $iterator->key();
    print_r($iterator->current());
    $iterator->next();
}
```

Listing 10-7: Using the methods in the Iterator interface to traverse an iterable object

You begin by calling the rewind method to ensure that you are at the start of the result set. The call to valid controls the while loop so that it continues only as long as there is another record to retrieve. In our implementation, the key returned by the key method will be a number; it is displayed here simply for demonstration purposes. The method current returns the record that the result set currently points to. Finally, a call to next advances the record pointer.

You've probably used foreach loops in many different circumstances (most likely with arrays), but you may not have given much thought to what goes on in the background. Listing 10-7 shows what happens in a foreach loop. At the start of the loop an implicit call is made to the rewind method, ensuring that you are at the beginning and that the first record is ready to be displayed. If there is a valid record you can enter the loop with the record pointer pointing to the current row. The record pointer is then advanced—by making an implicit call to next—and the process is repeated until the end of the record set is reached.

ITERATOR METHODS

We'll seldom use the iterator methods directly. We're implementing this interface so that we can use a MySQLResultSet within a foreach loop. In a sense, these methods are magic because they are invoked in the background by the foreach construct in much the same way that the __toString method of the MySQLException class is invoked when a MySQLException object is displayed. Any object used within a foreach loop must devise its own implementation of the iterator methods. The implementation will differ depending upon the nature of the object—an iterator that traverses file directories will differ significantly from a result set iterator, for example, but all objects that implement a specific interface will exhibit common behaviors. The point of an interface is that it guarantees the existence of specific methods without specifying what exactly these methods should do.

Implementation

To implement an interface, you need to indicate inheritance in your class definition. When inheriting from a class you use the keyword extends, but when inheriting from an interface you use implements. Your class definition now reads

```
class MySQLResultSet implements Iterator
```

Implementing an interface also requires that all methods be defined.

In this particular case you must add the five methods of an iterator, as well as the new data members currentrow, valid, and key, to your existing class. The currentrow member will hold the value(s) of the current row. The member valid is a Boolean that indicates whether there is a current row. The member key simply functions as an array subscript.

Five New Methods

The first three methods that your new class MySQLResultSet inherits from the Iterator interface are straightforward accessor methods that return the value of the newly added data members, like so:

```
public function current (){
    return $this->currentrow;
}
public function key (){
    return $this->key;
}
```

```
public function valid (){
    return $this->valid;
}
```

The method current returns the value of the current record if there is one; key returns its array subscript; and valid returns true unless the record pointer is positioned at the end of the record set. The more interesting methods, however, are next and rewind. First, let's look at the next method:

```
public function next (){
    if($this->currentrow = ❶mysql_fetch_array($this->result)){
        $this->valid = true;
        $this->key++;
    }else{
        $this->valid = false;
    }
}
```

In this code, you see that next attempts to retrieve the next row from ❶ the result set, and then resets the data members valid and key accordingly.

As you would expect, rewind resets the record pointer to the beginning of the result set after first checking that the number of rows is greater than 0. This method must also maintain the valid and key data members. The data member valid indicates whether there is a current row, and key is reset to 0.

Here's the rewind method:

```
public function rewind (){
    if(mysql_num_rows($this->result) > 0){
        if(❶mysql_data_seek($this->result, 0)){
            $this->valid = true;
            $this->key = 0;
            $this->currentrow = mysql_fetch_array($this->result);
        }
    }else{
        $this->valid = false;
    }
}
```

This method works because your result set is buffered; it was created using the function mysql_query. Because a buffered result set stores all rows in memory, ❶ the record pointer can be repositioned.

NOTE   *An unbuffered result set uses a forward-only cursor, so it cannot use the mysql_data_seek function. Unbuffered result sets are discussed in both Chapter 15 and Chapter 16.*

What to Do with Flightless Birds

Flightless birds such as the emu and the ostrich are unquestionably birds, but they lack one defining characteristic of birds—flight. Like flightless birds, unbuffered result sets lack one characteristic of an iterator. Unbuffered result sets are unquestionably iterable, but they cannot be rewound.

When I introduced interfaces I defined them as classes that have methods but no body for those methods. A class that implements an interface must provide the body for every method of the interface. What, then, do you do with an unbuffered result set and the rewind method?

Just as flightless birds simply don't fly, an unbuffered result set can define a rewind method that does nothing.

NOTE *The problem of unwanted methods of an interface is not peculiar to PHP. Other OO languages such as Java circumvent this problem by using "adapter" classes that provide an empty implementation of unwanted methods and only require that desired methods be defined.*

Leaving a Method Undefined

If you implement an interface but don't define all of its methods, you'll receive a fatal error message. For example, if you try to use the MySQLResultSet class without defining the key method, you'll see a fatal error like this:

```
Class MySQLResultSet contains 1 abstract methods and must therefore be
declared abstract (Iterator::key)
```

Not the error you would expect, perhaps, but an error nonetheless, and an informative one at that. As you can see, even though you haven't implemented the key method, it hasn't gone away because it is inherited from the Iterator interface. (The key method is considered abstract because it has no implementation.)

There are two ways to eliminate this error message. The obvious one, of course, is to define the key method. However, you could also create error-free code by adding the modifier abstract to your class by changing the declaration class MySQLResultSet to abstract class MySQLResultSet.

You've just created your first *abstract class*, which is a class with one or more methods that lack an implementation. A *purely abstract class* is one in which all methods lack an implementation, as with all methods in an interface. The only difference between a purely abstract class and an interface is that it is defined as a class rather than as an interface.

NOTE *You cannot create an instance of an abstract class; you must inherit from it and implement the abstract method(s), as with an interface. You'll learn about abstract classes in the next chapter.*

Implementation and Access

By removing the key method and forcing an error we learned a few more things about OOP. Let's see what we can learn by changing the access modifier of the rewind method from public to private. Do this and preview the class in your browser. You should see this fatal error:

```
Access level to MySQLResultSet::rewind() must be public (as in class Iterator)
```

Not only must you implement all the methods of the Iterator interface, you cannot make access to those methods more restrictive. If you think about it this makes good sense. The foreach construct needs a public rewind method—it would not have access to a private rewind method.

However, you can make access less restrictive because doing so will not interfere with the way other classes expect your implementation to behave. For example, you could make protected methods public. (This rule applies in all cases of inheritance, not just to interfaces.)

Iterating Through a MySQLResultSet

In Chapter 9 you traversed your result set using a while loop and the getRow method like so:

```
while($row = $rs->getRow()){
    echo $row[0]." - ".$row[1];
    echo "<br />\n";
}
```

Because you've implemented the Iterator interface you can traverse your result set using a foreach loop. The while loop above is now replaced by this:

```
foreach($rs as $row ){
    echo $row[0]." - ".$row[1];
    echo "<br />\n";
}
```

As you can see, it is more difficult to implement the Iterator interface than it is to create a method suitable for use in a while loop. Although this may seem like a lot of pain for no gain, there are advantages to this approach. For example, we can iterate through a record set a number of times, by simply starting another foreach loop. The record pointer will be reset in the background without any action on your part. Had you used your original code, you would have had to write a rewind method and explicitly call it before repeating a while loop.

NOTE   *Learning about the Iterator interface is time well spent as a number of built-in classes and interfaces inherit from this interface. For example, there is a DirectoryIterator class— a versatile replacement for the DirectoryItems class you developed in the early chapters.*

Where to Go from Here

In this chapter we've improved on our original database classes by creating our own exception class. This, in turn, allowed us to take a completely OO approach to handling exceptions rather than simply trapping errors and terminating the application. We added the ability to use a MySQLResultSet in a foreach loop by implementing the Iterator interface, and we explored the concept of inheritance both for classes and for interfaces.

We've spent a lot of time creating database classes because they are useful tools for making websites dynamic. In the next chapter, we're going to take a detailed look at some of the concepts introduced here. After that we'll take a look at other ways to add content to a website dynamically.

11

ADVANCED OBJECT-ORIENTED PROGRAMMING CONCEPTS

The previous two chapters introduced a number of new object-oriented programming (OOP) concepts. In the interest of clarity, some topics were discussed in depth and others glossed over. While the content of those chapters is still fresh in your mind, let's return to some of the topics that were only touched upon briefly, namely abstract classes, the use of the static keyword, and the implications of type hinting.

Abstract Classes

In Chapter 10 we saw that if a derived class does not implement all the methods of an interface, then it must be declared abstract. Let's push this concept to the extreme and see what a completely abstract class might look like. Listing 11-1 shows the definition of such a class.

```
❶abstract class Bird{
  protected $plumage;
  protected $migratory;
  abstract public function __construct();
  abstract public function fly();
  abstract public function sing();
  abstract public function eat();
  abstract public function setPlumage($plumage);
  abstract public function getPlumage();
  abstract public function setMigratory($migratory);
  abstract public function getMigratory();
}
```

Listing 11-1: The definition of the abstract class Bird

As we saw in Chapter 10, any class that contains abstract methods must include ❶ the keyword abstract in its class declaration. That class may have any number of data members and any number of methods with or without an implementation. However, if a method lacks an implementation it must also be declared abstract.

The class in Listing 11-1 has data members declared as protected, making them available to derived classes. This class could be termed a pure abstract class because all of its methods are abstract. Note that all the methods of this class are declared public. Let's see why that is so.

Private Methods Can't Be Abstract

Methods identified as abstract cannot be private; they must be either public or protected. The reason is that an abstract private method is a contradiction in terms. Because an abstract class has undefined methods it cannot be instantiated (it only exists to be the parent of a derived class). A class with abstract private methods could never be implemented because private methods cannot be inherited. The same reasoning would apply to a final abstract method.

NOTE   *Recall that a final method cannot be changed in a derived class. An abstract method cannot be final because it must be overridden—i.e., changed.*

How does a pure abstract class, with no defined methods, differ from an interface? An interface may not have data members or a constructor. (This may change in future versions of PHP. There is some discussion of allowing interfaces to have constructors.) In order to turn the Bird class, shown in Listing 11-1, into an interface you would have to replace the keywords abstract class with interface and remove $plumage, $migratory, and the constructor. Although interface methods are effectively abstract, you still need to remove the abstract descriptor for each method.

Interface or Pure Abstract Class?

You now know the syntactic differences between interfaces and pure abstract classes, but when should you use one rather than the other? In general, it's probably better to use an interface than a pure abstract class because of the flexibility of interfaces. PHP doesn't allow multiple inheritance for classes; a child class may have only one parent class. However, you can implement any number of interfaces.

It makes more sense to use abstract classes when there is a mix of concrete and abstract methods. You can provide an implementation where identical, derived class behavior is expected, and you can provide an abstract method where behavior will differ. You could, of course, ignore methods for which you expect the behavior of derived classes to diverge, but by declaring a method abstract you ensure that it will be implemented in any derived class. You'll see how this can be used to your advantage in the following discussion of polymorphism.

Polymorphism

In Chapter 10 you created a MySQLException class by inheriting from Exception. Type hinting allowed you to easily distinguish different kinds of exceptions and made it possible to have more than one catch block. However, when using type hinting, you also had to order the catch blocks carefully to make sure that the child preceded the parent. Specifically, MySQLException had to precede Exception because a catch block that catches the Exception class will also catch any derived class. Because it is derived from Exception, MySQLException can be caught by an Exception catch block. A parent class can stand in for its children, but a child cannot stand in for its parent. (This may look like a drawback, but you'll soon see how it can be used to advantage.)

Controlling How Functions Are Used

Type hinting can give a programmer more control over the way that a function is used. Suppose you derive a Canary class and a Lark class from the Bird class shown in Listing 11-1. You could pass either a canary or a lark to the function in Listing 11-2.

```
function doSomething(Bird $b){
    //do something
    $b->sing();
    //do something else
}
```

Listing 11-2: A function that uses type hinting to specify a Bird object

Even though the Bird class is an abstract class that cannot be instantiated, you can use it to type hint the argument to this function in exactly the same way that catch blocks are type hinted.

In Listing 11-2, type hinting prohibits passing anything but a bird to the function—passing any other object or a primitive will result in an error. In this way, a programmer can restrict the way that a function is used. With properly ordered catch blocks you used type hinting to catch *specific* kinds of exceptions. The doSomething function does the converse; it catches *any* kind of Bird. The ability to pass any kind of Bird to this function without knowing the specific kind beforehand, with the expectation that it will behave as it is supposed to behave, is known as *polymorphism*. The parent takes on the characteristics of the child.

As you are aware, PHP is a weakly-typed language. In the strictest sense, polymorphism requires a strongly-typed language such as Java or C++. In these languages, whenever a variable is declared or used as a function parameter, it is declared as a specific data type. In PHP, type hinting a parameter doesn't define the data type but merely filters for acceptable types. In terms of the code in Listing 11-2, Bird doesn't define the type of $b; it simply blocks out all other types. If this is the case, then $b is a variable like any other PHP variable, of no specific type. It is a variant that becomes a type through assignment. You don't in fact have a Bird class with the capability of performing the methods of whatever child class is passed. You have only the child class itself. Hence it is disputable whether PHP in fact supports polymorphism.

Regardless of whether PHP is truly polymorphic, the combination of type hinting and abstract methods is a powerful tool. The former guarantees a certain kind of object, and the latter guarantees the implementation of particular methods. For these reasons you can be sure that any object passed to the doSomething function will implement the sing method. The declaration of an abstract sing method ensures that you can't have a bird that doesn't sing and the type hint ensures that only a bird may be passed to this function.

NOTE *Type hinting is optional in all situations except catch blocks. A variable's data type in a catch must be specified, and it must be an Exception or a class derived from Exception. Type hinting applies to objects only (although as of PHP 5.1, arrays can also be type hinted). Type-hinted code is also self-documenting because it makes the programmer's intentions explicit. (We'll discuss this topic in greater detail in Chapter 14.)*

Static Classes

In Chapter 9, you used a static data member to allow only one instance of the MySQL database class. Whenever an attempt was made to create an instance of this class, you were able to test the value of the $instances variable to ensure that no other instances existed. This test works because a variable declared as static is available to all instances of a class (or in this case, would-be instances).

Static Math Classes

The ability to create classes that are entirely static allows us to encapsulate a set of related unchanging data members and methods. Mathematics is an ideal candidate for this kind of class because constants, such as pi and the way of calculating the absolute value of a number, do not change. Listing 11-3 shows what a piece of the static Math class might look like.

```
final class Math{
  const PI = M_PI;
  static public function abs($num){
    return abs($num);
  }
  static public function sqrt($num){
    return sqrt($num);
  }
}
echo Math::PI;
echo '<br />';
echo Math::abs(-4.15);
echo '<br />';
echo Math::sqrt(9);
```

Listing 11-3: A portion of the code for a static Math class

So far you have only seen the keyword final applied to methods. When used as a class modifier, it defines a class that cannot be the parent of any other class. A well-defined Math class should have no need of subclasses—it should not need to be extended and none of its methods overridden. The keyword final ensures this.

The Math class contains mathematical constants and performs mathematical functions. The constant data member PI can be displayed by using the class name and the scope resolution operator. Static methods are called in a similar fashion. The use of the class name and the scope resolution operator rather than the arrow operator indicates that the properties or methods belong to the class as a whole and not to any specific instance. Therefore, it is illegal to reference the pseudo-variable $this from within a static method because $this refers to the current instance. A static method, by definition, is not tied to any specific instance.

NOTE *Unlike some other OO languages, PHP does not allow the keyword static to be applied to a class as a whole. For example, attempting to declare final static class Math will result in an error. Therefore, when I speak of a static class in PHP, I am using the term loosely. I really mean a class that has only static methods.*

Instances of Static Classes

Because the keyword static cannot be applied to a class, you can create an instance of a class even if that class has only static data members. For example, you can create an instance of the Math class from Listing 11-3:

```
$m = new Math();
echo $m->sqrt(9);
```

Although this coding style is not recommended, an instance of the Math class will be created, and no error or notice will occur when you call the static method sqrt against this instance.

This will offend OO purists, because static methods belong to the class as a whole and should not be called against instances. However, changes are afoot for PHP when it comes to calling dynamic methods statically—"We will make calling a dynamic function with the static call syntax E_FATAL."[1]

Preventing Instantiation of a Static Class

It is quite easy to prevent your Math class from being instantiated. Simply add a constructor like the following:

```php
public function __construct(){
    throw new Exception("Static class - instances not allowed.");
}
```

This constructor will throw an exception if there is an attempt to create an instance of the Math class.

We could go on to create a complete Math class by adding all the appropriate methods, mostly wrapper methods for existing PHP functions, as we did for the absolute value function and the square root function shown in Listing 11-3. All in all, we can create a reasonable facsimile of a static class.

It makes sense to create a static Math class for an entirely OO language such as Java (after all, there's no procedural way, in this case, of calling mathematical functions), but the need to create static classes in a hybrid language such as PHP is questionable. In this case the static methods of a static Math class provide the equivalent of global functions that already exist in the PHP function library.

Although the value of static classes may be moot, you'll see shortly that static methods can be very useful.

Design Patterns

Originally, design patterns were templates used for solving common architectural problems, but they have also been applied to computer programming. Patterns are somewhat akin to abstract classes or interfaces, but are even less specific, providing only a general description of a solution.

The Singleton Pattern

One well-known and well-documented design pattern is the *singleton pattern*, a pattern that ideally suits the database class you created in Chapters 9 and 10. As the name implies, this pattern is used where only one instance of a class is wanted.

Your implementation of the MySQLConnect class uses a static variable and throws an exception if there is an attempt to construct more than one instance of the class. A more conventional implementation of the singleton pattern might use a private constructor and a static method to return a class

---

[1] PHP Developers Meeting, minutes (Paris, November 11–12, 2005), available at www.php.net/ ~derick/meeting-notes.html. (Accessed April 4, 2006.)

instance. Let's revise the MySQLConnect class to highlight the usefulness of static methods. (I'll outline only the major changes here; download the code if you want to see them all.)

To begin with, the static data member designed to keep track of the number of instances becomes a static data member for holding a reference to the class instance.

```
private static $instance = NULL;
```

The constructor still creates a connection, but the access modifier is changed from public to private and the test for existing instances is removed.

```
private function __construct($hostname, $username, $password){
    if(!$this->connection = mysql_connect($hostname, $username, $password)){
        throw new MySQLException(mysql_error(), mysql_errno());
    }
}
```

Because the constructor has been declared as private, you can only invoke it from within the class. This may seem like an impossibility (how do you get inside a class that you can't create?), but a static method provides the means, as shown in Listing 11-4.

```
static public function getInstance($hostname, $username, $password){
    //instance must be static in order to be referenced here
    if(self❶::$instance == NULL ){
        self::$instance = new MySQLConnect❷($hostname, $username, $password);
        return self::$instance;
    }else{
        $msg = "Close the existing instance of the ".
            "MySQLConnect class.";
        throw new MySQLException($msg, self::ONLY_ONE_INSTANCE_ALLOWED);
    }
}
```

Listing 11-4: Static method for returning an instance

In order to reference ❶ the instance handle inside a static method, the handle itself must be static. If no instance exists, the constructor ❷ is called and the returned object is copied into the static class variable $instance. The getInstance method then returns a reference to this static data member.

Now, instead of directly creating an instance of the MySQLConnect class by calling the constructor, you invoke the static getInstance method to perform that task for you.

```
$instance = MySQLConnect::getInstance('localhost', 'user', 'password');
```

It was noted earlier that static methods can only reference static data members. Conversely, static methods are prohibited from referencing regular data members. This makes sense when you remember that regular data members belong to and are created when objects are instantiated. By definition a static method does not require an object, so those non-static data members don't exist. Likewise, as you saw earlier, a static method cannot use the pseudo-variable $this, since $this refers to the current instance.

NOTE *A singleton class should also disallow clones. You'll see how this is done in Chapter 13.*

Which Implementation?

This revised MySQLConnect class has exactly the same functionality as the original. Apart from the way an instance is created, there is no other change to the interface of the MySQLConnect class. However, having a copy of the lone instance stored in a static class variable allows you to return that instance instead of throwing an exception, should an attempt be made to create a second instance. This is exactly what some implementations of a singleton database class do, but it is not always the desired behavior. What if the user wants to connect to a different server? For this reason, in the section "Making Other Connections" on page 68, we chose to force the user to close the current connection before creating a new one.

The coding style of the original implementation may be more direct and more readily understood, but having a reference to the class instance could prove useful in some circumstances. If the getInstance method receives a request to connect to the same host with the same username, why not return the current instance rather than throwing an exception?

Which version is preferable? It's up to you to decide.

Where to Go from Here

The keywords abstract and static and the ability to type hint add powerful capabilities that didn't exist prior to PHP 5. Creating abstract methods enforces specific kinds of behavior, and static methods and data members make the implementation of a singleton pattern both easy and effective. Type hinting makes the developer's intentions clear and programmatically enforces them.

These capabilities are not just syntactic icing on top of a procedural language; they are a robust implementation of a fully OO language. PHP may be unable to create a true static class, and whether it is truly polymorphic is debatable, but the issue for PHP is always functionality rather than language purity. There is no doubt that it does not suffer in this respect.

To this point we have created our own classes from scratch or inherited from existing ones defined in the Standard PHP Library (Iterator and Exception). PHP 5 includes many other classes besides those defined in the SPL. In the next chapter we'll use two of them, SimpleXMLElement and SOAPClient.

12

KEEPING IT FRESH

There's nothing quite like the excitement of discovering a new and interesting website. But this enthusiasm can quickly wane if, after a few visits, the content of the site hasn't changed at all. The primary way of adding new content to a website is by using dynamic, database-driven pages. That's why we've spent so much time discussing MySQL (and will later spend some time on SQLite). Another ideal way of keeping a site current and interesting is by using Rich Site Summary (RSS) feeds. RSS is a file format for web syndication that is widely used by various newsgroups but more commonly encountered in the form of a blog. An RSS file is an Extensible Markup Language (XML) formatted file that can be read using the SimpleXML extension to PHP 5. All you need in order to read an RSS feed is a little knowledge of how an RSS file is structured and an understanding of object-oriented programming (OOP). You'll be surprised at just how easy it is once you've grasped a few basics of XML.

The downside to having a large website with numerous pages is that it can be difficult for casual web surfers to find what they're looking for. For this reason I will also show you how to create a site-specific search. I'll do this using the Google Application Programming Interface (API) and the Simple Object Access Protocol (SOAP) extension to PHP. The Google API will allow us to tap into Google's search capabilities programmatically using the SOAP web service protocol. This protocol uses XML files over HTTP, so some familiarity with XML is required. If you don't know anything about XML, don't worry. You'll learn enough to get you started, and besides, you already know HTML so you're well on your way to understanding XML.

In this chapter you'll also have the opportunity to see how asynchronous JavaScript and XML (AJAX) can work in unison with PHP. We'll use AJAX to insert the Google search results, thus avoiding having to refresh the entire page. In situations where a page reload is overkill, using AJAX can greatly simplify the user interface to a website (though, of course, improper use can do the exact opposite).

The object-oriented (OO) programmer is ideally placed to program using SimpleXML and SOAP because, as you'll see, both extensions are entirely object-oriented. Like it or not, knowledge of OOP is a requirement for taking full advantage of these and many other extensions to PHP.

SimpleXML

In PHP 5 all XML support is now provided by the libxml2 XML toolkit. By default PHP 5 supports SimpleXML, but if libxml2 is not installed on your machine or the version number is lower than 2.5.10, go to www.xmlsoft.org and download the latest version. (You can use the PHP function phpinfo to check which version of libxml is running on your server.) Without going into too many details, suffice it to say that support for XML has been brought into line with the standards defined by the World Wide Web Consortium (W3C). Unified treatment of XML under libxml2 makes for a more efficient and more easily maintained implementation of XML support.

Support for XML is much improved in PHP 5, in terms of both performance and functionality. The SimpleXML extension makes full use of the libxml2 toolkit to provide easy access to XML, and as a quick way of converting XML documents to PHP data types.

XML

Since an RSS document is an XML document, you need some understanding of the basics of XML if you want to be able to read a feed. XML is a markup language that is similar in many ways to HTML—this should come as no surprise given that both HTML and XML have a common heritage in Standard Generalized Markup Language (SGML). As a web developer, even if you have never seen an XML file before, it will look familiar, especially if you are coding to the XHTML standard. XML makes use of tags or elements enclosed by angle brackets. Just as in HTML, a closing tag is differentiated from an opening tag by preceding the element name with a forward slash. Also like

HTML, tags can have attributes. The major difference between XML tags and HTML tags is that HTML tags are predefined; in XML you can define your own tags. It is this capability that puts the "extensible" in XML. The best way to understand XML is by examining an XML document. Before doing so, let me say a few words about RSS documents.

RSS

Unfortunately there are numerous versions of RSS. Let's take a pragmatic approach and ignore the details of RSS's tortuous history. With something new it's always best to start with a simple example, and the simplest version of RSS is version 0.91. This version has officially been declared obsolete, but it is still widely used, and knowledge of its structure provides a firm basis for migrating to version 2.0, so your efforts will not be wasted. I'll show you an example of a version 0.91 RSS file—in fact, it is the very RSS feed that we are going to use to display news items in a web page.

Structure of an RSS File

As we have done earlier with our own code, let's walk through the RSS code, commenting where appropriate.

The very first component of an XML file is the version declaration. This declaration shows a version number and, like the following example, may also contain information about character encoding.

```
<?xml version="1.0" encoding="iso-8859-1"?>
```

After the XML version declaration, the next line of code begins the very first element of the document. The name of this element defines the type of XML document. For this reason, this element is known as the *document element* or *root element*. Not surprisingly, our document type is RSS. This opening element defines the RSS version number and has a matching closing tag that terminates the document in much the same way that <html> and </html> open and close a web page.

```
<rss version="0.91">
```

A properly formatted RSS document requires a single channel element. This element will contain metadata about the feed as well as the actual data that makes up the feed. A channel element has three required sub-elements: a title, a link, and a description. In our code we will extract the channel title element to form a header for our web page.

```
<channel>
  <title>About Classical Music</title>
  <link>http://classicalmusic.about.com/</link>
  <description>Get the latest headlines from the About.com Classical Music
Guide Site.</description>
```

The language, pubDate, and image sub-elements all contain optional meta-data about the channel.

```
<language>en-us</language>
<pubDate>Sun, 19 March 2006 21:25:29 -0500</pubDate>
<image>
    <title>About.com</title>
    <url>http://z.about.com/d/lg/rss.gif</url>
    <link>http://about.com/</link>
    <width>88</width>
    <height>31</height>
</image>
```

The item element that follows is what we are really interested in. The three required elements of an item are the ones that appear here: the title, link, and description. This is the part of the RSS feed that will form the content of our web page. We'll create an HTML anchor tag using the title and link elements, and follow this with the description.

```
<item>
    <title>And the Oscar goes to...</title>
    <link>http://classicalmusic.about.com/b/a/249503.htm</link>
    <description>Find out who won this year's Oscar for Best Music...
    </description>
</item>
```

Only one item is shown here, but any number may appear. It is common to find about 20 items in a typical RSS feed.

```
</channel>
</rss>
```

Termination of the channel element is followed by the termination of the rss element. These tags are properly nested one within the other, and each tag has a matching end tag, so we may say that this XML document is *well-formed*.

Reading the Feed

In order to read this feed we'll pass its URI to the simplexml_load_file function and create a SimpleXMLElement object. This object has four built-in methods and as many properties or data members as its XML source file.

```php
<?php
//point to an xml file
$feed = "http://z.about.com/6/g/classicalmusic/b/index.xml";
//create object of SimpleXMLElement class
$sxml = simplexml_load_file($feed);
```

We can use the attributes method to extract the RSS version number from the root element.

```
foreach ($sxml->attributes() as $key => $value){
  echo "RSS $key $value";
}
```

The channel title can be referenced in an OO fashion as a nested property. Please note, however, that we cannot reference $sxml->channel->title from within quotation marks because it is a complex expression. Alternate syntax using curly braces is shown in the comment below.

```
echo "<h2>" . $sxml->channel->title . "</h2>\n";
//below won't work
//echo "<h2>$sxml->channel->title</h2>\n";
//may use the syntax below
//echo "<h2>{$sxml->channel->title}</h2>\n";echo "<p>\n";
```

As you might expect, a SimpleXMLElement supports iteration.

```
//iterate through items as though an array
foreach ($sxml->channel->item as $item){
  $strtemp = "<a href=\"$item->link\">".
    "$item->title</a> $item->description<br /><br />\n";
  echo $strtemp;
}
?>
</p>
```

I told you it was going to be easy, but I'll bet you didn't expect so few lines of code. With only a basic understanding of the structure of an RSS file we were able to embed an RSS feed into a web page.

The SimpleXML extension excels in circumstances such as this where the file structure is known beforehand. We know we are dealing with an RSS file, and we know that if the file is well-formed it must contain certain elements. On the other hand, if we don't know the file format we're dealing with, the SimpleXML extension won't be able to do the job. A SimpleXMLElement cannot query an XML file in order to determine its structure. Living up to its name, SimpleXML is the easiest XML extension to use. For more complex interactions with XML files you'll have to use the Document Object Model (DOM) or the Simple API for XML (SAX) extensions. In any case, by providing the SimpleXML extension, PHP 5 has stayed true to its origins and provided an easy way to perform what might otherwise be a fairly complex task.

Site-Specific Search

In this portion of the chapter we are going to use the Google API and the SOAP extension to create a site-specific search engine. Instead of creating our own index, we'll use the one created by Google. We'll access it via the SOAP protocol. Obviously, this kind of search engine can only be implemented for a site that has been indexed by Google.

Google API

API stands for Application Programming Interface—and is the means for tapping into the Google search engine and performing searches programmatically. You'll need a license key in order to use the Google API, so go to www.google.com/apis and create a Google account. This license key will allow you to initiate up to 1,000 programmatic searches per day. Depending on the nature of your website, this should be more than adequate. As a general rule, if you are getting fewer than 5,000 visits per day then you are unlikely to exceed this number of searches.

When you get your license key, you should also download the API developer's kit. We won't be using it here, but you might want to take a look at it. This kit contains the XML description of the search service in the Web Service Definition Language (WSDL) file and a copy of the file `APIs_Reference.html`. If you plan to make extensive use of the Google API, then the information in the reference file is invaluable. Among other things, it shows the legal values for a language-specific search, and it details some of the API's limitations. For instance, unlike a search initiated at Google's site, the maximum number of words an API query may contain is 10.

AJAX

This is not the place for a tutorial on AJAX (and besides, I'm not the person to deliver such a tutorial) so we're going to make things easy on ourselves by using the prototype JavaScript framework found at http://prototype.conio.net. With this library you can be up and running quickly with AJAX.

You'll find a link to the prototype library on the companion website or you can go directly to the URL referenced above. In any case, you'll need the `prototype.js` file to run the code presented in this part of the chapter.

Installing SOAP

SOAP is not installed by default. This extension is only available if PHP has been configured with `--enable-soap`. (If you are running PHP under Windows, make sure you have a copy of the file `php_soap.dll`, add the line `extension = php_soap.dll` to your `php.ini` file, and restart your web server.)

If configuring PHP with support for SOAP is not within your control, you can implement something very similar to what we are doing here by using the NuSOAP classes that you'll find at http://sourceforge.net/projects/nusoap. Even if you do have SOAP enabled, it is worth becoming familiar with NuSOAP not only to appreciate some well-crafted OO code, but also to realize just how much work this extension saves you. There are more than 5,000 lines of code in the `nusoap.php` file. It's going to take us fewer than 50 lines of code to initiate our Google search. Furthermore, the SOAP client we create, since it's using a built-in class, will run appreciably faster than one created using NuSOAP. (The NuSOAP classes are also useful if you need SOAP support under PHP 4.)

The SOAP Extension

You may think that the SOAP extension is best left to the large shops doing enterprise programming—well, think again. Although the "simple" in SOAP is not quite as simple as the "simple" in SimpleXML, the PHP implementation of SOAP is not difficult to use, at least where the SOAP client is concerned. Other objects associated with the SOAP protocol—the SOAP server in particular—are more challenging. However, once you understand how to use a SOAP client, you won't find implementing the server intimidating.

In cases where a WSDL file exists—and that is the case with the Google API—we don't really need to know much about a SOAP client beyond how to construct one because the SOAP protocol is a way of executing remote procedure calls using a locally created object. For this reason, knowing the methods of the service we are using is paramount.

A SOAP Client

To make use of a web service, we need to create a SOAP client. The first step in creating a client for the Google API is reading the WSDL description of the service found at http://api.google.com/GoogleSearch.wsdl. SOAP allows us to create a client object using the information in this file. We will then invoke the doGoogleSearch method of this object. Let's step through the code in our usual fashion beginning with the file dosearch.php. This is the file that actually does the search before handing the results over to an AJAX call.

The first step is to retrieve the search criterion variable.

```
<?php
$criterion = ❶@htmlentities($_GET["criterion"], ENT_NOQUOTES);
if(strpos($criterion, "\"")){
    $criterion = stripslashes($criterion);
    echo "<b>$criterion</b>"."</p><hr style=\"border:1px dotted black\" />";
}else{
    echo "\"<b>$criterion</b>\"."</p><hr style=\"border:1px dotted black\" />";
}
echo "<b>$criterion</b></p><hr style=\"border:1px dotted black\" /><br />";
```

Wrapping the retrieved variable in a call to ❶ htmlentities is not strictly necessary since we're passing it on to the Google API and it will doubtless be filtered there. However, filtering input is essential for security and a good habit to cultivate.

Make It Site-Specific

A Google search can be restricted to a specific website in exactly the same way that this is done when searching manually using a browser—you simply add site: followed by the domain you wish to search to the existing criterion. Our example code searches the No Starch Press site, but substitute your own values for the bolded text.

```
//put your site here
$query = $criterion . " site:www.yoursite.com";
//your Google key goes here
$key = "your_google_key";
```

In this particular case we are only interested in the top few results of our search. However, if you look closely at the code, you'll quickly see how we could use a page navigator and show all the results over a number of different web pages. We have a $start variable that can be used to adjust the offset at which to begin our search. Also, as you'll soon see, we can determine the total number of results that our search returns.

```
$maxresults = 10;
$start = 0;
```

A SoapClient Object

Creating a SOAP client may throw an exception, so we enclose our code within a try block.

```
try{
    $client = new SoapClient("http://api.google.com/GoogleSearch.wsdl");
```

When creating a SoapClient object, we pass in the WSDL URL. There is also an elective second argument to the constructor that configures the options of the SoapClient object. However, this argument is usually only necessary when no WSDL file is provided. Creating a SoapClient object returns a reference to GoogleSearchService. We can then call the doGoogleSearch method of this service. Our code contains a comment that details the parameters and the return type of this method.

```
/*
doGoogleSearchResponse  doGoogleSearch (string key, string q, int
start, int  maxResults, boolean filter, string restrict, boolean
safeSearch, string lr, string ie, string oe)
*/
    $results = $client->doGoogleSearch($key, $query, $start, $maxresults,
false, '', false, '', '', '');
```

This method is invoked, as is any method, by using an object instance and the arrow operator. The purpose of each argument to the doGoogleSearch method is readily apparent except for the final three. You can restrict the search to a specific language by passing in a language name as the third-to-last parameter. The final two parameters indicate input and output character set encoding. They can be ignored; use of these arguments has been deprecated.

The doGoogleSearch method returns a GoogleSearchResult made up of the following elements:

```
/*
GoogleSearchResults are made up of
documentFiltering, searchComments, estimatedTotalResultsCount,
estimateIsExact,  resultElements, searchQuery, startIndex,
endIndex, searchTips, directoryCategories, searchTime
*/
```

Getting the Results

We are only interested in three of the properties of the GoogleSearchResult: the time our search took, how many results are returned, and the results themselves.

```
$searchtime = $results->searchTime;
$total = $results->estimatedTotalResultsCount;
if($total > 0){
```

The results are encapsulated in the resultElements property.

```
//retrieve the array of result elements
$re = $results->resultElements;
```

ResultElements have the following characteristics:

```
/*
ResultElements are made up of summary, URL, snippet,
title, cachedSize, relatedInformationPresent,
hostName, directoryCategory, directoryTitle
*/
```

We iterate through the ResultElements returned and display the URL as a hyperlink along with the snippet of text that surrounds the search results.

```
    foreach ($re as $key => $value){
        $strtemp = "<a href= \"$value->URL\"> ".
            " $value->URL</a> $value->snippet<br /><br />\n";
        echo $strtemp;
    }
    echo "<hr style=\"border:1px dotted black\" />";
    echo "<br />Search time: $searchtime seconds.";
}else{
  echo "<br /><br />Nothing found.";
}
}
```

Our call to the Google API is enclosed within a try block so there must be a corresponding catch. A SOAPFault is another object in the SOAP extension. It functions exactly like an exception.

```
catch (SOAPFault $exception){
    echo $exception;
}
?>
```

Testing the Functionality

View the dosearch.php page in a browser, add the query string ?criterion=linux to the URL, and the SoapClient will return a result from Google's API. You should get site-specific search results that look something like those shown in Figure 12-1.

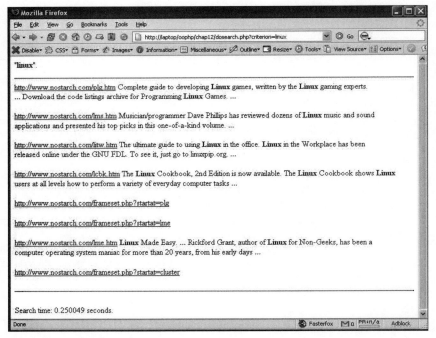

Figure 12-1: Search results

There are hyperlinks to the pages where the search criterion was found, along with snippets of text surrounding this criterion. Within the snippet of text the criterion is bolded.

As already mentioned, this is not the solution for a high-traffic site where many searches will be initiated. Nor is it a solution for a newly posted site. Until a site is indexed by Google, no search results will be returned. Likewise, recent changes to a site will not be found until the Googlebot visits and registers them. However, these limitations are a small price to pay for such an easy way to implement a site-specific search capability.

Viewing the Results Using AJAX

Viewing the results in a browser confirms that the code we have written thus far is functional. We're now ready to invoke this script from another page (search.html) using AJAX. The HTML code to do this is quite simple:

```
Search the No Starch Press site: <br />
<❶input type="text" id="criterion" style="width:150px" /><br />
<❷input class="subbutton" style="margin-top:5px;width:60px;" type="button"
value="Submit" onclick="javascript:call_server();" />
<h2>Search Results</h2>
<❸div id="searchresults" style="width:650px; display: block;">
Enter a criterion.
</div>
```

There's ❶ a textbox for input and ❷ a submit button that, when clicked, invokes the JavaScript function, call_server. The results of our search will be displayed in ❸ the div with the id searchresults.

To see how this is done, let's have a look at the JavaScript code:

```
<script type="text/javascript" language="javascript" src=
❶"scripts/prototype.js">
</script>
<script type="text/javascript" >
/*******************************************************************/
// Use prototype.js and copy result into div
/*******************************************************************/
function call_server(){
    var obj = ❷$('criterion');
    if(❸not_blank(obj)){
        ❹$('searchresults').innerHTML = "Working...";
        var url = ❺'dosearch.php';
        var pars = ❻'criterion='+ obj.value;
        new ❼Ajax.Updater( 'searchresults', url,
        {
            method: 'get',
            parameters: pars,
            ❽onFailure: report_error
        });
    }
}
```

We must first include ❶ the prototype.js file because we want to use the Ajax.Updater object contained in that file. This file also gives us the capability of simplifying JavaScript syntax. The reference to ❷ criterion using the $() syntax is an easy substitute for the document.getElementById DOM function. The if statement invokes a JavaScript function ❸ to check that there is text in the criterion textbox. If so, the text in ❹ the searchresults div is overwritten using the innerHTML property, indicating to the user that a search is in progress. The URL that performs the search is identified (❺), as is ❻ the search criterion. These variables are passed to the constructor of ❼ an

Ajax.Updater, as is ❽ the name of the function to be invoked upon failure. The Ajax.Updater class handles all the tricky code related to creating an XMLHttpRequest and also handles copying the results back into the searchresults div. All you have to do is point it to the right server-side script.

There are a number of other Ajax classes in the prototype.js file and the $() syntax is just one of a number of helpful utility functions. The companion website has a link to a tutorial on using prototype.js should you wish to investigate further.

Complex Tasks Made Easy

I've detailed just one of the services you can access using SOAP. Go to www.xmethods.net to get an idea of just how many services are available. Services range from the very useful—email address verifiers—to the relatively arcane—Icelandic TV station listings. You'll be surprised at the number and variety of services that can be implemented just as easily as a Google search.

In this chapter you've seen how easy it is to create a SOAP client using PHP. We quickly got up and running with AJAX, thanks to the prototype.js framework, and you've seen that PHP and AJAX can work well together. Reading a news feed was simpler still. These are all tasks that rely heavily on XML, but minimal knowledge of this technology was required because PHP does a good job of hiding the messy details.

Would You Want to Do It Procedurally?

Knowledge of OOP is a requirement for anything beyond trivial use of the SimpleXML and SOAP extensions to PHP. OOP is not only a necessity in order to take full advantage of PHP, but it is by far the easiest way to read a feed or use SOAP. A procedural approach to either of the tasks presented in this chapter is not really feasible. Any attempt would unquestionably be much more difficult and require many, many more lines of code. Using built-in objects hides the complexity of implementing web services and makes their implementation much easier for the developer.

13

MORE MAGIC METHODS

So far we have come across the magic methods __construct, __destruct, and __toString, and have discussed them in detail. The remaining magic methods are __autoload, __call, __clone, __get, __set, __sleep, __wakeup, __unset, and __isset.[1] As you might expect, they only make sense in the context of object-oriented programming (OOP).

The syntactic element common to all magic methods is that they begin with a double underscore. They are all also usually invoked indirectly rather than directly. As we have seen, the __construct method of a class is invoked when we use the new operator and a class name. If we have a class called MyClass that defines a constructor, the statement $m = new MyClass(); indirectly calls the __construct method of this class.

However, the fact that all magic methods are called indirectly masks important differences between them. Having a uniform constructor for every class yields benefits when a parent constructor needs to be called, but there is

---

[1] There is also a magic method_set_state, invoked by a call to the var_dump function. At this point there is minimal documentation regarding this method. For more information see http://php.net/var_export.

no intrinsic need for this method to be magic. For example, in Java, constructors bear the name of the class with no serious negative consequences. On the other hand, destructors are a necessity and would seem to have to be magic. They are not invoked by any action of the developer, but automatically when an object goes out of scope. Then there's the __toString method, which is called implicitly whenever an object is displayed using print or echo—a convenience method more than anything else. In any case, the point is that the reasons for providing magic methods are various and in each case worth examining.

In this chapter we will look at those magic methods that we haven't yet discussed. Related and complementary methods will be discussed together.

__get and __set

To set the context for this discussion, remember that we spent some time discussing accessor, or set and get methods, in Chapter 6. There I argued that instance variables should be made private and only retrieved or changed through accessor methods. Doing otherwise violates the object-oriented (OO) principle of data hiding (or encapsulation if you prefer) and leaves instance variables exposed to inadvertent changes.

PHP 5 introduces magic set and get methods for undefined instance variables. Let's see what this means by looking at an example. Suppose you have a class, Person, devoid of any data members or methods, defined as follows:

```
class Person{
}
```

PHP allows you to do the following:

```
$p = new Person();
$p->name = "Fred";
$p->street = "36 Springdale Blvd";
```

Even though name and street data members have not been declared within the Person class, you can assign them values and, once assigned, you can retrieve those values. This is what is meant by *undefined instance variables*. You can create magic set and get methods to handle any undefined instance variables by making the following changes to the Person class, as shown in Listing 13-1.

```
class Person{
    protected ❶$datamembers = array();
    public function ❸__set($variable, $value){
        //perhaps check value passed in
        $this->datamembers[$variable] = $value;
    }
    public function __get($variable){
        return $this->datamembers[$variable];
    }
}
$p = new Person();
$p->❷name = "Fred";
```

Listing 13-1: Defining magic set and get methods

You add ❶ an array to your class and use it to capture any undeclared instance variables. With these revisions, assigning a value to an undeclared data member called ❷ name invokes ❸ the __set method in the background, and an array element with the key name will be assigned a value of "Fred." In a similar fashion the __get method will retrieve name.

Is It Worth It?

Magic set and get methods are introduced as a convenience, but it is certainly questionable whether they are worth the effort. Encouraging the use of undefined data members can easily lead to difficulties when debugging. For instance, if you want to change the value of the name data member of your Person class instance, but misspell it, PHP will quietly create another instance variable. Setting a nonexistent data member produces no error or warning, so your spelling error will be difficult to catch. On the other hand, attempting to use an undefined method produces a fatal error. For this reason, declaring data members to be private (or protected), and ensuring that they are only accessible through declared accessor methods, eliminates the danger of accidentally creating a new unwanted data member. Using declared data members means fewer debugging problems.

Undeclared data members also seem contrary to the principles of OOP. Although you might argue that encapsulation has been preserved because undeclared data members are only accessed indirectly through the magic methods, the real point of accessor methods is to control how instance variables are changed or retrieved. The comment inside the __set method (//perhaps check value passed in) in Listing 13-1 suggests that such controls could be implemented, but in order to do so you would need to know the variable names beforehand—an impossibility given that they are undeclared. Why not just set up properly declared data members?

Allowing undeclared data members also undermines another basic concept of OOP, namely inheritance. It's hard to see how a derived class might inherit undeclared instance variables.

One might argue, though, that these magic methods make PHP easier to use and this convenience offsets any of the disadvantages. After all, the original and continuing impetus behind PHP is to simplify web development. Allowing undeclared data members in PHP 5 is perhaps a necessary evil because doing so keeps backward compatibility with PHP 4. While it's easy to criticize magic set and get methods, in Chapter 16, when discussing the PDORow class, you'll see that these methods can come in very handy.

__isset and __unset

PHP 5.1.0 introduces the magic methods __isset and __unset. These methods are called indirectly by the built-in PHP functions isset and unset. The need for these magic methods results directly from the existence of magic set and get methods for undeclared data members. The magic method __isset will be called whenever isset is used with an undeclared data member.

Suppose you want to determine whether the name variable of your Person instance in Listing 13-1 has been set. If you execute the code isset($t->name);, the return value will be false. To properly check whether an undeclared data member has been set, you need to define an __isset method. Redo the code for the Person class to incorporate a magic __isset method (see Listing 13-2).

```
class Person{
    protected $datamembers = array();
    private $declaredvar = 1;
    public function __set($variable, $value){
        //perhaps check value passed in
        $this->datamembers[$variable] = $value;
    }
    public function __get($variable){
        return $this->datamembers[$variable];
    }
    function __isset($name){
        return isset($this->datamembers[$name]);
    }
    function getDeclaredVariable(){
      return $this->declaredvar;
    }
}
$p = new Person();
$p->name = 'Fred';
echo '$name: '. isset($p->❶name). '<br />';//returns true
$temp = $p->getDeclaredVariable();
echo '$declaredvar: '. isset(❷$temp). '<br />';//returns true
true
true
```

Listing 13-2: The Person class with a magic __isset method

Calling isset against the undeclared data member ❶ name will return true because an implicit call is made to the __isset method. Testing whether ❷ a declared data member is set will also return true, but no call, implicit or otherwise, is made to __isset. We haven't provided an __unset method, but by looking at the __isset method you can easily see how an undeclared variable might be unset.

You have __isset and __unset methods only because there are magic set and get methods. All in all, in most situations, it seems simpler to forget about using undeclared data members, and thereby do away with the need for magic set and get methods and their companion __isset and __unset methods.

__call

The magic method __call is to undeclared methods what __get and __set are to undeclared data members. This is another magic method provided as a convenience. At first, it is a little difficult to imagine what an undeclared method might be and what use it might have. Well, here's one way that this method can prove useful. Suppose you wanted to add to the functionality of the MySQLResultSet class defined in Chapters 9 and 10, so as to retrieve the current system status in this fashion:

```
//assume $rs is an instance of MySQLResultSet
$rs->stat();
```

You could just create a wrapper method for the existing MySQL function, mysql_stat, as you did when creating other methods of this class. For example, the existing getInsertId method simply encloses a call to mysql_insert_id. You could do exactly the same thing with mysql_stat. However, the more versatile option is to add a __call method similar to the following code:

```
public function __call($name, $args){
    $name = "mysql_". $name(;
    if(function_exists($name)){
        return call_user_func_array($name, $args);
    }
}
```

When you call the stat method against a MySQLResultSet object, the method name, stat, is passed to the __call method where mysql_ is prepended. The mysql_stat method is then invoked by the call_user_func_array function. Not only can you call the mysql_stat function, but once __call is defined you can call any MySQL function against a MySQLResultSet class instance by simply using the function name, minus the leading mysql_, and supplying any required arguments. This magic method does away with the need for writing wrapper methods for existing MySQL function, and allows them to be "inherited." If you're already familiar with the MySQL function names it also makes for easy use of the class.

However, this magic method is not quite as convenient as it might seem at first glance. Functions such as mysql_fetch_array that require that a result set resource be passed even though the class is itself a result set resource make nonsense of the whole notion of an object—why should an object need to pass a copy of itself in order to make a method call? On the other hand, this is an easy and natural way to incorporate functions such as mysql_stat and mysql_errno that don't require any arguments, or functions such as mysql_escape_string that require primitive data types as arguments. If properly used, this convenience method seems much more defensible than the __set and __get methods.

__autoload

The __autoload function is a convenience that allows you to use classes without having to explicitly write code to include them. It's a bit different from other magic methods because it is not incorporated into a class definition. It is simply included in your code like any other procedural function.

Normally, to use classes you would include them in the following way:

```
require 'MySQLResultSet.php';
require 'MySQLConnect.php';
require 'PageNavigator.php';
require 'DirectoryItems.php';
require 'Documenter.php';
```

These five lines of code can be replaced with the following:

```
function __autoload($class) {
    require $class '.php';
}
```

The __autoload function will be invoked whenever there is an attempt to use a class that has not been explicitly included. The class name will be passed to this magic function, and the class can then be included by creating the filename that holds the class definition. Of course, to use __autoload as coded above, the class definition file will have to be in the current directory or in the include path.

Using __autoload is especially convenient when your code includes numerous class files. There is no performance penalty to pay—in fact, there may be performance improvements if not all classes are used all the time. Use of the __autoload function also has the beneficial side effect of requiring strict naming conventions for files that hold class definitions. You can see from the previous code listing that the naming conventions used in this book (i.e., combining the class name and the extension .php to form the filename) will work fine with __autoload.

__sleep and __wakeup

These magic methods have been available since PHP 4 and are invoked by the variable handling functions serialize and unserialize. They control how an object is represented so that it can be stored and recreated. The way that you store or communicate an integer is fairly trivial, but objects are more complex than primitive data types. Just as the __toString method controls how an object is displayed to the screen, __sleep controls how an object will be stored. This magic method is invoked indirectly whenever a call to the serialize function is made. Cleanup operations such as closing a database connection can be performed within the __sleep method before an object is serialized.

Conversely, __wakeup is invoked by unserialize and restores the object.

__clone

Like the constructor, __clone is invoked by a PHP operator, in this case clone. This is a new operator introduced with PHP 5. To see why it is necessary, we need to take a look at how objects are copied in PHP 4.

In PHP 4 objects are copied in exactly the same way that regular variables are copied. To illustrate, let's reuse the Person class shown in Listing 13-1 (see Listing 13-3).

```
$x = 3;
$y = $x;
$y = 4;
echo $x. '<br />';
echo $y. '<br />';
$obj1 = new Person();
$obj1->name = 'Waldo';
$obj2 ❶= $obj1;
$obj2->name = 'Tom';
echo $obj1->name. '<br />';
echo $obj2->name;
```

Listing 13-3: Using the assignment operator under PHP 4

If the code in Listing 13-3 is run under PHP 4, the output will be as follows:

```
3
4
Waldo
Tom
```

The assignment of $obj1 to $obj2 (❶) creates a separate copy of a Person just as the assignment of $x to $y creates a separate integer container. Changing the name attribute of $obj2 does not affect $obj1 in any way, just as changing the value of $y doesn't affect $x.

In PHP 5, the assignment operator behaves differently when it is used with objects. When run under PHP 5, the output of the code in Listing 13-3 is the following:

```
3
4
Tom
Tom
```

For both objects the name attribute is now Tom.

Where's Waldo?

In PHP 5, the assignment of one object to another creates a reference rather than a copy. This means that $obj2 is not an independent object but another means of referring to $obj1. Any changes to $obj2 will also change $obj1. Using the assignment operator with objects under PHP 5 is equivalent to assigning by reference under PHP 4. (You may recall our use of the assignment by reference operator in Chapter 4.)

In other words, in PHP 5

```
//PHP 5
$obj2 = $obj1;
```

achieves the same result as

```
//PHP 4
$obj2 =& $obj1;
```

The same logic applies when an object is passed to a function. This is not surprising, because there is an implicit assignment when passing a variable to a function. Under PHP 4, when objects are passed to functions, the default is to pass them by value, creating a copy in exactly the same way as with any primitive variable. This behavior was changed in PHP 5 because of the inefficiencies associated with passing by value. Why pass by value and use up memory when, in most cases, all that's wanted is a reference? To summarize, in PHP 5, when an object is passed to a function or when one object is assigned to another, it is assigned by reference. However, there are some situations where you do want to create a copy of an object and not just another reference to the same object. Hence the need to introduce the clone operator.

NOTE *If you are porting PHP 4 code to a server running PHP 5, you can remove all those ungainly ampersands associated with passing an object by reference or assigning it by reference.*

clone

To understand the clone operator, let's use the Person class again, adding a few more lines of code to Listing 13-3 to create the code in Listing 13-4.

```
if ($obj1 === $obj2)❶{
    echo '$obj2 equals $obj1.<br />';
}
$obj3 = ❷clone $obj1;
echo 'After cloning ';
if ($obj1 === $obj3){
    //this code will execute
    echo '$obj3 equals $obj1.<br />';
}else{
    echo '$obj3 does not equal $obj1.<br />';
}
$obj3->name = ❸'Waldo';
echo 'Here\'s '. $obj1->name. '.<br />';
echo 'Here\'s '. $obj3->name. '.<br />';
$obj2 equals $obj1
After cloning $obj3 does not equal $obj1.
❹Here's Tom.
Here's Waldo.
```

Listing 13-4: Finding Waldo

Remember that in Listing 13-3 $obj1 was assigned to $obj2, so the identity test conducted here shows ❶ that they are equal. This is because $obj2 is a reference to $obj1. After $obj1 ❷ is cloned to create $obj3 in Listing 13-4, the test for identity produces a negative result.

The name attribute of your newly cloned object ❸ is changed, and ❹ the output shows that this change does not affect the original object. In PHP 5, cloning an object makes a copy of an object just as the assignment operator does in PHP 4.

You may have supposed that in our search for Waldo we lost sight of our ultimate goal. Not true. Now that you understand the clone operator, you can make sense of the __clone method. It is invoked in the background when an object is cloned. It allows you to fine-tune what happens when an object is copied. This is best demonstrated using an aggregate class as an example.

Aggregate Classes

An *aggregate class* is any class that includes a data member that is itself an object. Let's quickly create a Team class as an example. This class has as a data member, an array of objects called players. The class definitions for the Player class and the Team class are shown in Listing 13-5.

```
class Player{
    private $name;
    private $position;
    public function __construct($name){
        $this->name = $name;
    }
    public function getName(){
        return $this->name;
    }
    public function setPosition($position){
        $this->position = $position;
    }
}
class Team{
    private $players = array();
    private $name;
    public function __construct($name){
        $this->name = $name;
    }
    public function addPlayer(Player $p){
        $this->players[] = $p;
    }
    public function getPlayers(){
        return $this->players;
    }
    public function getName(){
        return $this->name;
    }
```

```
    public function setName($name){
        $this->name = $name;
    }
}
```

Listing 13-5: The Team aggregate class

Let's create a player, add him to a team, and see what happens when you clone that object (see Listing 13-6).

```
$rovers = new Team('Rovers');
$roy = new Player('Roy');
$roy->setPosition('striker');
$rovers->addPlayer($roy);
$reserves = clone $rovers;
$reserves->setName('Reserves');
//changes both with __clone undefined
❶$roy->setPosition('midfielder');
echo $rovers->getName(). ' ';
print_r($rovers->getPlayers());
echo '<br /><br />';
echo $reserves->getName(). ' ';
print_r($reserves->getPlayers());
```

Listing 13-6: Cloning an aggregate object

Setting ❶ a player's position after the clone operation changes the value of position for the player in both objects. Outputting the players array proves this—Roy's position is the same for both objects (see Listing 13-7).

```
Rovers Array ( [0] => Player Object ( [name:private] => Roy [position:private]
=> midfielder ) )
Reserves Array ( [0] => Player Object ( [name:private] => Roy
[position:private] => midfielder ) )
```

Listing 13-7: Undesired result of cloning

Because player is an object, the default behavior when making a copy is to create a reference rather than an independent object. For this reason, any change to an existing player affects the players array for both Team instances. This is known as a shallow copy and in most cases doesn't yield the desired result. The magic clone method was introduced in order to deal with situations such as this. Let's add a __clone method to the Team class so that each team has a separate array of players. The code to do this is as follows:

```
public function __clone(){
    $newarray = array();
    foreach ($this->players as $p){
        $newarray[] = ❶clone $p;
    }
    $this->players = $newarray;
}
```

While looping through the array of players ❶ each individual player is cloned and added to a new array. Doing this creates a separate array for the cloned team. After making these changes, running the code in Listing 13-6 now yields this output:

```
Rovers Array ( [0] => Player Object ( [name:private] => Roy [position:private]
=> ❶midfielder ) )
Reserves Array ( [0] => Player Object ( [name:private] => Roy
[position:private] => ❶striker ) )
```

Changing a player originally added to the $rovers has no effect on the player array in ❶ the cloned $reserves object. This is the result you want. The magic clone method allows you to define what happens when an object is cloned. Using the terminology of other OO languages, the __clone method is a copy constructor. It's up to the developer to decide what's appropriate for any particular class, but as a general rule, a __clone method should always be defined for aggregate classes for the exact reasons shown in the sample code—normally the same variable isn't shared among different instances of a class. (That's what static data members are for.)

A Get Method for Object Data Members of an Aggregate Class

When I first introduced accessor methods in Chapter 5, I noted that one of the advantages of a get method over direct access to a public data member was that accessor methods return a copy rather than an original. This is not true when the data members are themselves objects—by default objects are returned by reference. In the interests of data protection, it is usually better to return a copy using the clone operator. With this in mind, let's rewrite the getPlayers method originally shown in Listing 13-5, shown here in Listing 13-8.

```
public function getPlayers(){
    $arraycopy = array();
    foreach ($this->players as $p){
        $arraycopy[] = clone $p;
    }
    return $arraycopy;
}
```

Listing 13-8: Returning a copy of an object

The array returned by this version of the getPlayers method is only a copy so changes made to it will have no effect on the data member, $players. If you need to make changes to the players array a set method will have to be written. Doing so is a fairly straightforward matter so I'll leave that up to you.

The fact that objects are passed by reference also has implications for how objects are added to an aggregate class. For instance, consider the player Roy who is added to the team Rovers in Listing 13-6. Any changes made to the variable $roy will change the first element of the $players array in the $rovers object. This may or may not be what's wanted. If not, then players should be cloned before being added to the players array.

The addPlayer method of the Team class could be rewritten as:

```php
public function addPlayer(Player $p){
    $newplayer = clone $p;
    $this->players[] = $newplayer;
}
```

The Team class now has complete control over any player added. This will doubtless be the implementation preferred by any Team manager.

NOTE *The fact that PHP 5 returns a reference to an object rather than a copy may have serious implications for aggregate objects written under PHP 4 and running under PHP 5. Objects formerly returned by value will now be returned by reference, breaking encapsulation.*

No Clones Allowed

As you saw when we discussed the singleton class in Chapter 11, in some cases it may make sense to disallow copies altogether. This can be done by implementing code such as the following:

```php
public final function __clone(){
    throw new Exception('No clones allowed!');
}
```

Making this method final ensures that this behavior can't be overridden in derived classes, and making it public displays a clear error message when there is an attempt at cloning. Making the __clone method private would also disallow cloning but displays a less explicit message: Access level must be public.

A Note About Overloading

On the PHP website the __set, __get, and __call methods are referred to as *overloaded methods*. Within the context of OOP, an overloaded method is one that has the same name as another method of the same class but differs in the number or type of arguments—methods with the same name but a different "signature." Because PHP is a typeless language and doesn't really care how many arguments are passed, this kind of overloading is an impossibility. In PHP, overloading usually refers to methods that perform a variety of different tasks.

Languages such as C++ also support something called *operator overloads*. For example, a programmer can define what the "greater than" operator means when two objects of the same class are compared. Support for such features has been described as "syntactic sugar" because, most of the time, operator overloads are not strictly necessary—the same effect could be achieved by writing a method rather than overloading an operator. However, operator overloads can be convenient and intuitive. It makes more sense to write:

```
if($obj1 > $obj2)
```

than

```
if($obj1->isGreaterThan($obj2))
```

The __toString method, while it is not an operator overload, offers a convenience similar to that of an operator overload. It is certainly nice to be able to control what is displayed to the screen when an object is echoed.

PHP supports operator overloading for clone and, as you have seen, this is not syntactic sugar but a matter of necessity. The same can be said of the __sleep and __wakeup methods because, as with destructors, the circumstances under which these methods are invoked aren't always under the direct control of the developer.

All other magic methods are there for convenience so would perhaps qualify as "syntactic sugar." I won't repeat the opinions expressed earlier about __set and __get or press the point. After all, PHP places a high premium on user convenience, aiming to get the job done quickly and easily. Undoubtedly, this is the reason for its success. If PHP's aim was language purity, OO or otherwise, it probably wouldn't still be with us.

14

CREATING DOCUMENTATION USING THE REFLECTION CLASSES

In Chapter 4, I introduced a simple class called DirectoryItems. You may remember what it does, but you probably can't remember the specific methods. With a user-defined class, looking up forgotten methods usually means rooting through the class definition file. This can take a long time, especially for large classes. For an internal class you can go to http://php.net to look up the information you need. But there are more than 100 internal classes and interfaces, and their documentation is scattered throughout the PHP site. Wouldn't it be useful to have a central repository of documentation for all classes?

Finding documentation is one problem, but the quality of documentation is another, equally important, problem. Most developers know the value of accurately commented code, but when you are in the middle of coding, the meaning of your code always seems crystal clear, so comments appear superfluous. Besides, there's always the ultimate excuse for the absence of internal documentation—you want to keep file size small to reduce download time.

This is often the situation with internal documentation, but external documentation fares no better. It doesn't make sense to write it as you go because things always change, but, by the time you've finished coding, documentation is the furthest thing from your mind. You're ready to move on to something else.

This chapter offers a solution to the two problems of ready availability and quality of documentation. We're going to create a documentation class derived from a new set of classes introduced in PHP 5, the reflection group. You'll learn how to generate documentation dynamically that will fully describe methods and data members and that will incorporate properly formatted internal comments for user-defined classes.

What Are the Reflection Classes?

In Chapter 10, before implementing the Iterator interface, you had to understand its methods. To create a class that will do your documenting for you, you need to become familiar with the *reflection classes*. This group of classes was created for the express purpose of introspecting other classes. These classes make it possible to examine the properties of other classes by retrieving metadata about classes; you can even use them to examine the reflection classes themselves.

Reflection provides information about the modifiers of a class or interface—whether that class is final or static, for example. It can also reveal all the methods and data members of a class and all the modifiers applied to them. Parameters passed to methods can also be introspected and the names of variables exposed. Through reflection it is possible to automate the documentation of built-in classes or user-defined classes. It turns out that the central repository of information about classes was right in front of us all the time. PHP can tell us all about itself through the mirror of the reflection classes.

The Reflection Group of Classes

The reflection group of classes or Application Programming Interface (API) is made up of a number of different classes and one interface, shown here:

```
class Reflection
interface Reflector
class ReflectionException extends Exception
class ReflectionFunction implements Reflector
class ReflectionParameter implements Reflector
class ReflectionMethod extends ReflectionFunction
class ReflectionClass implements Reflector
class ReflectionObject extends ReflectionClass
class ReflectionProperty implements Reflector
class ReflectionExtension implements Reflector
```

We won't be concerned with every class in the reflection API, but a general overview will help put things in perspective. Looking at this list, you may suppose that the Reflection class is the parent class of all the reflection classes, but there is actually no class ancestor common to all reflection classes. On the other hand, the Reflector interface is shared by all classes except Reflection and ReflectionException. As far as class hierarchies are concerned, ReflectionMethod extends ReflectionFunction, ReflectionObject extends ReflectionClass, and ReflectionException extends Exception.

Our concern is with objects, so we won't spend any time on the method ReflectionFunction. ReflectionObject shares all the methods of ReflectionClass; the only difference between these classes is that ReflectionObject takes a class instance rather than a class name as a parameter—using an instance, you can introspect a class without knowing anything about it, even its name. The class ReflectionException is derived from Exception, a class we've already examined.

We're principally interested in Reflection, ReflectionClass, ReflectionMethod, ReflectionParameter, and ReflectionProperty.

The Reflection Class

The Reflection class has two static methods: export and getModifierNames. We'll discuss getModifierNames later in this chapter, but let's take a look at the export method—a quick way to introspect a class—to get a taste of what Reflection can tell us. Reflection requires a ReflectionClass object as the parameter to the export method. Let's use the SOAPFault class as an example, since we recently encountered it in Chapter 12. The export method is static. As you'll recall from Chapter 11, static methods are invoked by using the class name and the scope resolution operator. Here's the code to export this class:

```
Reflection::export(new ReflectionClass('SOAPFault'));
```

In this example, a class name is passed to the ReflectionClass constructor, and the resultant object is the argument to the export method of the Reflection class. The output of the export method is shown in Listing 14-1.

```
Class [ <internal:soap> class SoapFault extends ❶Exception ] {
- Constants [0] {
}
- Static properties [0] {
}
- Static methods [0] {
}
- ❷Properties [4] {
  Property [ <default> protected $message ]
  Property [ <default> protected $code ]
  Property [ <default> protected $file ]
  Property [ <default> protected $line ]
}
```

```
-  ❸Methods [9] {
   Method [ <internal> <ctor> public method __construct ] {
   }
   Method [ <internal> public method __toString ] {
   }
   Method [ <internal> final private method __clone ] {
   }
   Method [ <internal> final public method getMessage ] {
   }
   Method [ <internal> final public method getCode ] {
   }
   Method [ <internal> final public method getFile ] {
   }
   Method [ <internal> final public method getLine ] {
   }
   Method [ <internal> final public method getTrace ] {
   }
   Method [ <internal> final public method getTraceAsString ] {
   }
  }
 }
}
```

Listing 14-1: Exporting SOAPFault

The export method gives a quick overview of a class. As you can see, SOAPFault extends ❶ the Exception class and possesses all ❷ the properties of Exception. Its methods are ❸ Exception class methods. This is exactly the sort of thing we want the reflection classes to do for us.

The ReflectionClass Class

The export method is quick and easy; but what if you want more information in a user-friendly format? The place to begin is with the ReflectionClass class, which you'll extend to create a Documenter class.

NOTE   *There are nearly 40 methods of ReflectionClass. Often, the methods' names clearly indicate their purpose. For instance, isInterface determines whether you are introspecting a class or an interface. We will only examine those methods that are of particular interest.*

Methods of ReflectionClass

The getMethods and getProperties methods play an important role in class documentation. Invoking getMethods returns an array of ReflectionMethod objects. Invoking getProperties returns an array of ReflectionProperty objects. These methods and the objects returned make it possible to fully describe a class's methods and data members.

You will recall that I promised we'd use internal comments when documenting a class. If internal comments are properly formatted, the getDocComment method of ReflectionClass can be used to incorporate them directly into your documentation.

Fortunately, `ReflectionMethod` and `ReflectionProperty` also have `getDocComment` methods, so method-level and data member–level comments can also be included.

NOTE *Those of you familiar with PEAR (PHP Extension and Application Repository) and phpDocumentor or the Java utility `Javadoc` will already know the proper format for internal comments.*

ReflectionMethod and ReflectionParameter

`ReflectionMethod` objects contain all the information you need to fully describe a method. By using this object you can document the modifiers of a method; you can use its `getParameters` method to return an array of `ReflectionParameter` objects, which is essential for describing a method's parameters.

A `ReflectionParameter` object will give you the number of parameters, their names, and any default values. You can even determine whether a parameter is a specific type of object if it is type hinted—yet another good reason to use type hinting.

There is one respect in which you might find the `ReflectionMethod` class wanting, however. Sometimes it's important to know what a method returns; for example, when using the `getMethods` method, it is essential to know that an array of `ReflectionMethod` objects is returned. Since you can type hint parameters and retrieve this information it would be nice to do the same with returned values. However, because PHP is a weakly-typed language, it's not surprising that this capability is not supported, so be sure to document return types in your comments where appropriate.

NOTE *Type hinting return values is planned for PHP 6, so perhaps we can expect support for this capability in future versions of the reflection classes.*

ReflectionProperty

The `getProperties` method of `ReflectionClass` is similar to the `getMethods` method. It returns an array of `ReflectionProperty` objects that can be queried in much the same way as `ReflectionMethod` objects. (Determining whether default values exist for data members poses some challenges; more about this shortly.)

Built-in Functions

We've looked at the principal classes and methods of the reflection classes, but there are some built-in PHP functions that can also be helpful when documenting classes. Most of the functions in the Class/Object group have been effectively, if not explicitly, deprecated in PHP 5 precisely because there are now reflection classes that do a superior job. However, a number of functions, such as `get_declared_classes` and `is_object`, continue to be useful.

What Format Do You Want?

One of the major reasons for documenting classes is to make them easier for a client programmer to use. Because the client programmer is primarily interested in the public methods of a class (he wants to know how to use the class, not how it works), you should sort methods and data members by visibility, giving priority to those with public visibility.

If you have ever used a plain text editor to write code you know that syntax highlighting greatly improves readability. For this reason, the ability to change the appearance of keywords is also a desirable characteristic to incorporate into your class.

You've been acquainted with the capabilities of various reflection classes, and now have a fair idea of what kind of off-the-shelf functionality is available as well as what you will have to customize. You're in a good position to begin extending `ReflectionClass`.

The Documenter Class

We won't be looking at each and every line of code in this class, but to help put the following comments in context you might want to download the code now. The export method of `Reflection` gave us a rough idea of the kind of information we would like to see (refer to Listing 14-1). Now let's discuss the `Documenter` class in terms of how class information will be displayed.

Describing the Documenter Class

At the very minimum you need basic information about a class. The `getFullDescription` method combines existing `ReflectionClass` methods to create a string that matches the actual class declaration.

```php
public function getFullDescription(){
    $description = "";
    if($this->isFinal()){
        $description = "final ";
    }
    if($this->isAbstract()){
        $description = "abstract ";
    }
    if($this->isInterface()){
        $description .= "interface ";
    }else{
        $description .= "class ";
    }
    $description .= $this->name . " ";
    if($this->getParentClass()){
        $name = $this->getParentClass()->getName();
        $description .= "extends $name ";
    }
```

```
$interfaces = $this->❶getInterfaces();
$number = count($interfaces);
if($number > 0){
    $counter = 0;
    $description .= "implements ";
    foreach($interfaces as $i){
        $description .= $i->getName();
        $counter ++;
        if($counter != $number){
            $description .= ", ";
        }
    }
}
return $description;
}
```

This code calls a number of self-explanatory, inherited methods to build a class description. The only slight complication is that, because a class can implement more than one interface, ❶ the getInterfaces method returns an array, and so requires a foreach loop. When applied to the SoapFault class, the following string is returned by the getFullDescription method:

```
class SoapFault extends Exception
```

SoapFault is correctly identified as a class rather than an interface, it is neither final nor abstract, and its derivation from Exception is documented. This is exactly the same description that you saw in Listing 14-1 when you exported this class.

Describing Methods and Data Members

Since methods are more important than data members, let's next deal with how to adapt the reflection classes to document methods. Calling the getMethods method of the ReflectionClass class creates an array of ReflectionMethod objects. The visibility of each method can then be determined by the isPublic, isProtected, or isPrivate methods of the ReflectionMethod class.

However, you want to display methods sorted by visibility—basically, you want a getPublicMethods method and an identical method for displaying private and protected methods. In order to be able to retrieve an array of ReflectionMethod objects sorted by visibility, you are going to loop through all the methods in a class and create separate arrays of each type. Let's see how this is done.

```
private function createMethodArrays(){
    $methods = $this->getMethods();
    //ReflectionMethod array returned
    foreach($methods as $m){
        $name = $m->getName();
        if($m->isPublic()){
            $this->publicmethods[$name] = $m;
        }
```

```
        if($m->isProtected()){
            $this->protectedmethods[$name] = $m;
        }
        if($m->isPrivate()){
            $this->privatemethods[$name] = $m;
        }
    }
}
```

Again, the code is quite simple. An array of all methods of a class is retrieved using the inherited `ReflectionClass` method getMethods, and each `ReflectionMethod` object is stored in the appropriate associative array, using the method name as the array key.

Each array is a private variable with a public accessor method—the prescribed way for retrieving data members. For example, to examine the public methods of a class, you simply call getPublicMethods, which will return the array populated by createMethodArrays.

Data member arrays are created in exactly the same fashion. Your class has a createDataMemberArrays that uses the getProperties method inherited from the `ReflectionClass` to create an array of `ReflectionProperty` objects. You then query each `ReflectionProperty` object to create arrays of public, private, and protected data members. These arrays can, in turn, be retrieved using accessor methods.

The Constructor

The createDataMemberArrays method and the companion method for creating an array of methods are both private and called from within the constructor of the Documenter class.

```
public function __construct($name){
    parent::__construct($name);
    $this->createDataMemberArrays();
    $this->createMethodArrays();
}
```

Placement of the call to the parent constructor is noteworthy. Because createDataMemberArrays and createMethodArrays both invoke methods of the parent class, it is essential that the call to the parent constructor occur first. Doing otherwise results in calling methods on a not-yet-existent object.

Method and Data Member Modifiers

It is essential to know the access modifiers for methods and data members of a class. Both the `ReflectionMethod` and the `ReflectionParameter` classes have a getModifiers method that returns an integer with bit fields set to flag the different access modifiers. Your Documenter class has its own getModifiers method that converts these flags to their string equivalents using the static getModifierNames method of the Reflection class.

```
public function getModifiers($r){
    if($r ❶instanceof ReflectionMethod ||
        $r ❶instanceof ReflectionProperty){
        $arr = ❷Reflection::getModifierNames($r->getModifiers());
        $description = implode(" ", $arr );
    }else{
        $msg = "Must be ReflectionMethod or ReflectionProperty";
        throw new ReflectionException( $msg );
    }
    return $description;
}
```

You want to ensure that only ReflectionMethod objects or ReflectionProperty objects are passed into this method so you use the operator, ❶ instanceof. This operator was introduced with PHP 5 and replaces the now-deprecated function is_a. This operator allows you to restrict use of your method to classes that support the getModifiers method and to throw a ReflectionException if the wrong type of object is passed in.

When you pass the return value of getModifiers to ❷ the static method of the Reflection class, getModifierNames, a string array of all the modifiers is returned. A series of calls to isPublic, isStatic, and like methods would achieve the same result, but using getModifierNames is by far the most succinct way of getting the string values of method and data member modifiers.

NO COMMON ANCESTOR

You might think that ReflectionMethod and ReflectionProperty objects each have a getModifiers method because they share a common interface, Reflector, and, consequently, you could type hint the parameter to this method to check for an instance of this particular interface only. However, you would be mistaken. There are only two methods of the Reflector interface: export and __toString. As far as a common class heritage is concerned, ReflectionMethod derives from ReflectionFunction and ReflectionProperty has no parent class. So there is no common parentage. That said, the fact remains that checking for an instance of the Reflector class would achieve essentially the same result as checking for ReflectionFunction and ReflectionProperty—but for the wrong reasons. It is only fortuitous that both classes have a getModifiers method. Another way to screen for the correct class would be to introspect the variable $r to determine whether it has a getModifiers method.

As an interesting aside, when introspecting the methods of a built-in interface, the modifiers are always public and abstract. In Chapter 11 you saw that PHP prohibits the use of the modifier abstract when defining the methods of a user-defined interface, despite the fact that the methods of an interface must in fact be abstract.

Using the Documenter Class

That completes the description of the Documenter class. We will now use it in a web page to display information about all internal and user-defined classes. We'll create a sidebar of links to all existing classes and interfaces, and display detailed information in the main portion of the page. Again, we won't discuss every line of code, only those lines that are of special interest.

Creating a Sidebar of Classes and Interfaces

Let's create a sidebar that will display the names of all PHP classes as hyperlinks—fulfilling the promise of a central repository of information about all classes. Clicking a hyperlink will display documentation for this class in the main portion of your web page. The code to do this follows:

```
❶include 'MySQLResultSet.php';
include 'MySQLConnect.php';
include 'Documenter.php';
include 'PageNavigator.php';
$arr = ❷get_declared_classes();
natcasesort($arr);
$classname = ❸@$_GET["class"];
if(!isset($classname)){
    $classname = current($arr);
}
echo "<h4 style=\"background-color:#fff;\">Classes</h4>";
foreach($arr as $key => $value){
    echo "<a href=\"getclass.php❹?class=$value\">".
        "$value</a><br />";
}
```

In addition to built-in classes, any user-defined classes that have been loaded using ❶ an include or require statement will be retrieved when you call ❷ the get_declared_classes function. If no ❸ variable named class has been passed to this page, then $classname will default to the name of the first class in the array of declared classes. This $classname variable contains the class name that will be passed to the constructor of the Documenter class. Information about the specified class will be displayed in the center of the page. A foreach loop creates the list of hyperlinks to all available classes by creating ❹ a query string that includes the class name.

Your sidebar also displays links to all the declared interfaces. The code to do this is identical to the code to retrieve classes except that it calls the function get_declared_interfaces instead of get_declared_classes. Therefore this code will not be reproduced here.

Formatting Detailed Documentation

The MySQLException class is a derived class that has a variety of methods (see Figure 14-1), so use it as an example of how we would like the class documentation to look.

```
Name: MySQLException

Date: Jan-19-2006
PHP version: 5.1.2
Type: User-defined

class MySQLException extends Exception

/** For use with MySQLConnection and MySQLResultSet classes*/

Public Methods

public __construct ( $message, $errorno ) user-defined
/** Create new message for client errors then call parent
constructor */

public __toString ( ) user-defined
/** Override the parent method and only show error message*/

final public getMessage ( )

final public getCode ( )

final public getFile ( )

final public getLine ( )

final public getTrace ( )

final public getTraceAsString ( )

Private Methods

final private __clone ( )

Protected Data Members

protected message

protected code

protected file

protected line
```

Figure 14-1: Documentation format

Let's proceed by relating the code to this output. The web page that displays your documentation first creates an instance of the Documenter class:

```
❶try{
    $class = new Documenter($classname);
    echo "<h2>Name: ". $class->❷getName() . "</h2>\n";
    $today = ❸date("M-d-Y");
    echo "<p> Date: $today<br />";
    echo "PHP version: ". phpversion() . "<br />";
    echo "Type: ". $class->❹getClassType() . "<br /><br />\n";
    echo "<span class=\"fulldescription\">". $class->❺getFullDescription().
        "</span><br /><br />\n";
    echo $class->❻getDocComment() . "</p>\n";
    ...
}
```

Because creating an instance may throw a ReflectionException, you enclose your call to the constructor within ❶ a try block. You need to know which class we are documenting, so you display the class name by calling ❷ the inherited method getName. Knowing when documentation was created is important, so you display the date using ❸ the date function. Likewise with the PHP version number. Since you are mixing built-in and user-defined classes, specifying ❹ the class type will reduce confusion.

As you saw earlier in this chapter, ❺ the full class description identifies whether you are dealing with a class or an interface, and also details the class parentage. Because internal comments within the class file have been properly formatted, you can extract them using ❻ the getDocComment method. When this method is called against an instance of a class, it retrieves the comment that immediately precedes the class definition. Let's see how that's done.

Formatting Comments for the Documenter

The getDocComment method is fussy about what it will retrieve, so let's look at the format of the comments within an existing user-defined class. We'll continue using the MySQLException class as an example.

```
/** For use with MySQLConnection and MySQLResultSet classes */
class MySQLException extends Exception
{ ... }
```

A class-related, internal comment must meet the following conditions for the getDocComment method to work:

- It must immediately precede the class definition statement.

- It may run to any number of lines but must begin with a forward slash, followed by two asterisks, followed by white space, and be terminated by an asterisk and forward slash—in other words, exactly the format required by Javadoc.

The ReflectionFunction, ReflectionMethod, and ReflectionObject classes also support a getDocComment method. (As of PHP 5.1, the ReflectionProperty class also supports this method.) Exactly the same formatting rules apply. Again, internal comments must immediately precede what they document.

As you can see in Figure 14-1, the internal comments documenting the constructor are displayed immediately after the class description—as promised, the Documenter class incorporates internal comments. Unfortunately, getDocComment only applies to user-defined classes and user-defined methods or data members; comments cannot be extracted for internal classes.

Documenting Methods

As shown in Figure 14-1, method documentation is displayed immediately after the class description and comments. With a view to the client programmer, public methods are displayed immediately after the class name and description, followed by protected methods, and finally private methods. Because the MySQLException class has no protected methods, none are shown.

Methods of all levels of visibility are passed to the show_methods function to handle the details of displaying method descriptions. Here is the prototype for this function:

```
function show_methods(Documenter $d, $type, $arr)
```

One of the parameters of this function is an object. In PHP 4 you would want to ensure that this object was passed by reference by preceding the variable with & (an ampersand). As discussed in Chapter 13 in the section "__clone" on page 116, in PHP 5 all objects are automatically passed by reference, so there is no need to do this. This parameter is also type hinted, disallowing anything other than a Documenter object.

To summarize, this function displays the variable names of method parameters, type hints, and default values where applicable. Syntax highlighting has been used for the keywords describing each method—you can quickly see in Figure 14-1 that the getMessage method of the MySQLException class is both final and public. User-defined methods are flagged as such, and any internal comments are displayed.

NOTE *If you are running PHP 5.1 or higher, you can type hint the array passed to show_methods by changing the function prototype to read function show_methods(Documenter $d, $type, array $arr).*

Data Members

Data members are handled in much the same way as methods. Those with the least restrictive visibility are presented first. Again, keywords are highlighted. Even default values assigned to data members can be retrieved. Somewhat surprisingly, this is done using the getDefaultProperties method of ReflectionClass rather than by using a ReflectionProperty class method. As with methods, all modifiers are shown. The value of constants is retrieved using the ReflectionClass method getConstants.

Reflecting

The reflection classes make it easy to generate documentation for both internal and user-defined classes. Documentation can be created directly from the class files themselves, so any changes to the class are immediately reflected in the documentation—much easier than separately maintaining both code and documentation. Descriptions of methods and hints about class usage are invaluable not only for the client programmer but also for the class originator, especially when a few months have lapsed between creation of a class and its subsequent use. Class documentation can effortlessly incorporate internal comments as long as you simply pay a little attention to their format during coding.

15

EXTENDING SQLITE

SQLite comes packaged with PHP 5. It has advanced capabilities and a built-in object-oriented (OO) interface. Examining the classes and methods of SQLite is the ostensible reason for including this chapter—but that's not the only reason. SQLite is a great addition to PHP, but because MySQL is so entrenched, programmers tend to ignore SQLite.

Don't let the "Lite" in SQLite lead you to underestimate the capabilities of this database. Because it is bundled with PHP, there is no external server to worry about—think of it as "Lite" in the sense of "no extra baggage." In some situations it is the ideal database to use. Its advanced features can help simplify your code and create an application that outperforms other solutions.

In this chapter, we will develop a link management application using a class derived from the SQLite database class. A minimum of PHP version 5.0.5 is a requirement. (Prior to this version the SQLite database class is declared as final, so it cannot be extended.)

Brief Overview

Relevant sections of code will be reproduced here, but, as usual, the entire application is available for download on the companion website. The front end for this application will display alphabetically ordered website links, as shown in Figure 15-1.

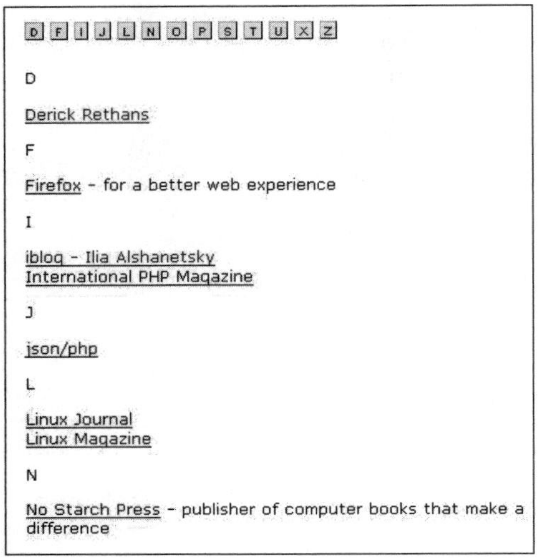

Figure 15-1: Resource links

An alphabetic navigation bar of hyperlinks will make any specific link easily accessible. Recently added links will be highlighted, making the list even more useful to regular visitors.

A submission form will allow visitors to suggest additional links. These links will not appear on the site until they have been reviewed. There will be a back end to review and maintain links.

Directory Structure

Because of the number of files in the download for this chapter, it's helpful to make a few comments about the way the files are organized. Download and decompress the files to follow along.

The front-end capabilities of this application are accessible from the links in the index.php file in the top level directory and the back end is found using the index.php file in the linkmanagement directory. On a production server the linkmanagement directory would be password protected but for ease of use that hasn't been done here.

For reasons of version compatibility, the database file itself is not included with the downloads. It should be installed in the dbdir directory. Version 2.8.17 of SQLite was used to test this application (but if you are already up and running with another version of SQLite you shouldn't run into any problems). Install the database from the db_install_script.php file (also included in the dbdir directory). Instructions on how to do this will follow shortly.

How It's Done

In this application we take advantage of some of SQLite's advanced capabilities. Both triggers and views will be used. A *trigger*, code that executes in response to an add, edit, or delete event, will be used to mimic a datestamp field—records will be automatically stamped whenever they are added or changed.

Views are a convenient way of storing queries and can replace tables in the FROM clause of a SELECT statement. They can also be used with triggers so that "updating" a view updates the associated table.

No database used in conjunction with PHP can escape comparison to MySQL. Where appropriate, I will point out differences in SQL syntax between SQLite and MySQL. Likewise, SQLite has a variety of different query methods. These will also be contrasted with MySQL functions.

As you have seen, throwing exceptions rather than trapping errors makes for cleaner code. SQLite has a built-in OO interface, and there is an SQLiteException class. However, only the SQLite database constructor throws exceptions. By extending the SQLite database class, we can override the query methods so that a failed query also throws an exception. This derived class will also include data verification methods that make use of metadata extracted from the database. This will be done by querying the sqlite_master table and through the use of pragmas. A *pragma* modifies the way the SQLite library works but can also be used to query the database structure. We're only interested in the second use.

A limited number of functions are available for use with SQLite's dialect of SQL. You'll see how this shortcoming can be overcome by creating user-defined functions (UDFs).

Getting Started

SQLite comes bundled with PHP 5, so all you have to do to install the database is run the db_install_script.php file.

However, if you do things this way you'll have to write code just to view your data or to examine the structure of your database. You might want to download the command-line version of SQLite instead. PHP 5, depending upon the subversion number, comes with SQLite versions 2.8.11 through 2.8.17. To find out which version is running on your system, display the results of the PHP function phpinfo in your browser and search for *SQLite*. For convenience, you might want to install the binary of sqlite in the same directory as your database.

Creating a database is as simple as typing the name of the SQLite executable file at the command line followed by the database name—for example, sqlite resources.sqlite. Doing so will run sqlite and create or open an existing database of the specified name. You can now create a table using SQL from the command line. However, let me make one more suggestion. At some point you will want to dump your database, and if you have created it from the command line the output won't be very readable.

If you use a text editor to format your CREATE TABLE statement and then redirect this file to the database, the results will be much more acceptable. Do this whenever you create tables, views, or triggers.

NOTE *Precompiled binaries for most operating systems are available at the SQLite download page (http://sqlite.org/download.html). For compatibility reasons it is important to get the command-line version number that matches the version incorporated into PHP. At the SQLite site you may have difficulty finding older versions. If there is no link to the version you require, enter the URL http://sqlite.org, followed by the version number you require, into the address bar of your browser—for example, http://www.sqlite.org/ sqlite-2_8_16.zip. You might get away with using a slightly higher or lower version number, but version 3 databases are an entirely different format from version 2, so do not attempt to use the version 3 command-line tool with a version 2 database.*

The database used in this application is called resources.sqlite and is stored in a subdirectory named dbdir. If you haven't already created it using the db_install_script.php file, you can do so by redirecting the dump.sql file from the command line in the following way:

```
sqlite resources.sqlite < dump.sql
```

A database dump is formatted as a transaction, so, if this command worked properly, you've already used one of SQLite's advanced features.

You can test that the database has been installed by executing a SELECT statement. Typing SELECT * FROM tblresources; should display all the records in the resources table.

Creating a Table

The SQL used to create the tblresources table in our database is shown in Listing 15-1.

```
CREATE TABLE tblresources(
    id INTEGER PRIMARY KEY,
    url VARCHAR(255) NOT NULL UNIQUE default '',
    email VARCHAR(70) NOT NULL default '',
    precedingcopy VARCHAR(100) NOT NULL default '',
    linktext VARCHAR(255) NOT NULL default '',
    followingcopy VARCHAR(255) NOT NULL default '',
    target VARCHAR(35) default '_blank',
    category VARCHAR(100) NOT NULL default '',
    theirlinkpage VARCHAR(100) default NULL,
    whenaltered TIMESTAMP default '0000-00-00',
    reviewed BOOLEAN default 0,
    whenadded DATE default '2006-05-05');
```

Listing 15-1: Creating a table

Let's have a look at the details.

To create a table with an autonumber field named id, the data type INTEGER is used in conjunction with PRIMARY KEY. This is equivalent to identifying a field as INTEGER auto_increment PRIMARY KEY in MySQL. In SQLite this field definition is the one exception to the rule that SQLite fields are typeless—otherwise all fields are strings. Creating fields as types other than string helps document the data types you are expecting but will not restrict the value entered. You can put a string into a float type field and a float into a Boolean. Further, specifying the length of a VARCHAR type field will not truncate data that exceeds the defined length. Any length of string can be entered into any field. Otherwise, the syntax for creating a table functions exactly as you might expect.

The field names used in creating this table are self-documenting, but a few comments are in order. A resource won't be displayed until the reviewed field is set to true. The field with the data type TIMESTAMP whenaltered will be maintained using a trigger as will the whenadded field.

Views

Views are stored SELECT queries. If you repeatedly use the same query, it is worthwhile creating it as a view.

To make resource links easily accessible, let's order them alphabetically and create hyperlinks to each letter of the alphabet. With this in mind, take a look at the alphabet view shown in Listing 15-2.

```
CREATE VIEW alphabet AS
    SELECT DISTINCT UPPER(SUBSTR(linktext,1,1)) AS letter
    FROM tblresources
    WHERE reviewed = 1
    ORDER BY letter;
CREATE VIEW specific_link AS
    SELECT id, url,
    (precedingcopy || ' ' || linktext || ' ' || followingcopy)
    AS copy
    FROM tblresources;
```

Listing 15-2: Views

The alphabet view creates a row of links as pictured at the top of Figure 15-1.

Rather than repeat the SQL statement that makes up the alphabet view, we can instead simply SELECT * FROM alphabet using the name of the view in the FROM clause.

The second view, specific_link, also shown in Listing 15-2, demonstrates how a view can be "updated" when used in conjunction with a trigger. We will return to this view in the following discussion about triggers, but do note the use of || as the string concatenation operator.

As you can see, SQLite defines its own string manipulation functions. For a complete list of functions and operators, see www.sqlite.org/lang_expr.html.

Triggers

For those programmers who pride themselves on their laziness, triggers are a wonderful thing. By creating a trigger you can get maximum effect with minimum effort.

Triggers are activated by an INSERT, DELETE, or UPDATE SQL statement. They are often used to maintain referential integrity and avoid orphaned records—for example, deleting an invoice might well trigger deletion of all related invoice items. We're going to create three triggers for our application: one to mimic a timestamp field, another to show the advantages of laziness, and finally a trigger to demonstrate how a view can be "updated."

The timestamp triggers are shown in Listing 15-3. They are activated whenever a record in the tblresources table is added or updated.

```
CREATE TRIGGER insert_resources AFTER INSERT ON tblresources
BEGIN
    UPDATE tblresources SET whenaltered = DATETIME('NOW','LOCALTIME')
    WHERE id = new.id;
END;
CREATE TRIGGER update_resources AFTER UPDATE ON tblresources
BEGIN
    UPDATE tblresources SET whenaltered = DATETIME('NOW','LOCALTIME')
    WHERE id = new.id;
END;
CREATE TRIGGER add_date AFTER INSERT ON tblresources
BEGIN
    UPDATE tblresources SET whenadded = DATE('NOW','LOCALTIME')
    WHERE id = new.id;
END;
CREATE TRIGGER delete_link INSTEAD OF DELETE ON specific_link
FOR EACH ROW
BEGIN
    DELETE FROM tblresources
    WHERE id = old.id;
END;
```

Listing 15-3: Triggers

There is no need to remember to update the whenaltered field each time a change is made to a record—the insert_resources and update_resources triggers will do this for you. The current date and time will be added in the background. Effectively, this field will now function like a MYSQL TIMESTAMP field.

Likewise with the add_date trigger, also shown in Listing 15-3. We want to highlight new links. This trigger makes it possible to capture the date a link is added. By using a trigger we don't have to worry about forgetting to maintain this field, and we don't have to write additional code each time a record is added.

Creating a trigger on a view is a convenient way of performing an "update" against a view. By themselves, views are not updatable. If you attempt to delete from a view that has no associated trigger, you'll get a warning like the following:

```
Warning: SQLiteDatabase::query() [function.query]: cannot
modify specific_link because it is a view...
```

We solved this problem in the trigger we created on the view specific_link shown in Listing 15-3. Because we used an INSTEAD OF clause, any attempt to delete from this view instead removes the appropriate record from the table, tblresources.

In this trigger we have specified FOR EACH ROW. Doing so is optional. A FOR EACH STATEMENT clause also exists but is not yet supported.

The WHERE clause of a trigger is somewhat intuitive but may cause some confusion. Using new.id to specify a newly inserted record and old.id for a deleted record clearly makes sense. Either old or new may be used when a record is updated.

Using triggers is very convenient, although the same effect could be achieved programmatically. But because triggers are embedded in the database, they are activated even when you make changes from the command line. Triggers help maintain the integrity of your database when it is modified outside of your application. Laziness has its rewards.

PHP Implementation of SQLite

For the most part, the OO methods of SQLite are exactly the same as the procedural functions. The only difference is that the leading sqlite is dropped and the studly caps naming convention is used in place of underscores (although some methods added in version 5.1 don't quite follow this rule). Method parameters are the same as those used with the procedural functions, except that there is no need to pass a resource handle since the object itself is the handle. A few functions are only available in a procedural form; these will be mentioned where appropriate.

There are three built-in, ready-to-use SQLite objects: an SQLite database, a buffered result set, and an unbuffered result set. All three classes will be used in this chapter, but the focus will be on the database class.

Extending SQLiteDatabase

One of the nice things about object-oriented programming (OOP) is exception handling. Procedural error trapping is not only tedious, it clutters up your code and can make it unreadable. Taking an OO approach and using exception handling sounds like the ideal solution—until you realize that the database constructor is the only method of all the SQLite classes that throws an exception. If you want to check for errors when creating result sets, you are stuck using procedural code. It looks like we're right back where we started.

We'll next discuss how this can be fixed.

Override the Query Methods

The simple solution to this problem is inheritance. On the surface, this would seem fairly straightforward: Create a class that extends SQLiteDatabase and override all the query methods. If errors arise within those overridden methods, simply throw an exception. In this way, the messy details of error trapping can be buried inside the class file and a single catch block can handle all errors. The first five methods in the class definition file shown in Listing 15-4 do exactly this.

```
///////////////////////////////////////////////////////////
//public functions related to queries
/**
Override function
*/
    public function query($strsql, $type = SQLITE_BOTH, &$err_msg = ''){
    //SQLiteResult query ( string query [, int result_type [, string &error_msg]] )
        if ( false === $result = parent::query($strsql, $type, $err_msg)){
            //no sql details with last error
            throw new SQLiteException (sqlite_error_string($this->lastError()));
        }
        return $result;
    }
///////////////////////////////////////////////////////////
/**
Override function
*/
    public function unbufferedQuery($strsql, $type = SQLITE_BOTH, &$err_msg = ''){
        //SQLiteUnbuffered unbufferedQuery ( string query [, int result_type [, string
&error_msg]] )
        if ( false === $result = parent::unbufferedQuery($strsql, $type, $err_msg)){
            throw new SQLiteException (sqlite_error_string($this->lastError()));
        }
        return $result;
    }
///////////////////////////////////////////////////////////
/**
Override function
*/
    public function singleQuery($strsql, $first_column = true, $bin_decode = false){
        //array sqlite_single_query ( resource db, string query [, bool first_row_only [, bool
decode_binary]] )
        if ( false === $result = parent::singleQuery($strsql, $first_column, $bin_decode)){
            throw new SQLiteException (sqlite_error_string($this->lastError()));
        }
        return $result;
    }
```

```
/////////////////////////////////////////////////////////////////
/**
Override function
*/
    public function queryExec($strsql, &$err_msg = ''){
        //bool queryExec ( string query [, string &error_msg] )
        if ( !parent::queryExec($strsql, $err_msg)){
            throw new SQLiteException (sqlite_error_string($this->lastError()));
        }
        return true;
    }
/////////////////////////////////////////////////////////////////
/**
Override function
*/
    public function arrayQuery($strsql, $type = SQLITE_BOTH, $bin_decode = false ){
    //array arrayQuery ( string query [, int result_type [, bool decode_binary]] )
        if ( false === $result = parent::arrayQuery($strsql, $type, $bin_decode)){
            throw new SQLiteException (sqlite_error_string($this->lastError()));
        }
        return $result;
    }
/////////////////////////////////////////////////////////////////
```

Listing 15-4: Extending the SQLiteDatabase class

In each case, the query method of the parent class, SQLiteDatabase, is redefined to include a test of the return value.

Error Messages

The comment immediately inside each method definition shows the method prototype as defined on the PHP site. This is especially useful because it shows the type of object returned. Some of the base class methods take an optional string reference argument (&$error_msg).

NOTE *In versions of PHP prior to 5.1, passing in this string reference results in this warning:* SQLiteDatabase::query() expects at most 2 parameters, 3 given.

The reason a third parameter is necessary is explained as follows (from http://php.net/sqlite_query):

> ... [$error_msg] will be filled if an error occurs.
>
> This is especially important because SQL syntax errors can't be fetched using the [sqlite_last_error()] function.

Quite true. The sqlite_last_error function returns an uninformative message: SQL logic error or missing database. Our code doesn't make use of this error message but this isn't an insurmountable problem. A more specific error message would certainly help in the debugging process, however. Fortunately, if you have warnings turned on while you are developing, you will get something more meaningful. Forcing a warning by referencing a nonexistent table results in the following, more specific, output:

```
Warning: SQLiteDatabase::query()[function.query]: no such
 table: tblnonexistent...
```

Query Methods

Look again at Listing 15-4. It includes the five methods for creating result sets. The buffered and unbuffered methods are fairly self-explanatory—you are probably quite familiar with the equivalent MySQL functions. However, MySQL (prior to the MySQL improved extension) has nothing to match the `singleQuery`, `queryExec`, or `arrayQuery` methods. Let's look at these methods in more detail.

The `singleQuery` method is a recent addition, and the PHP site warns that it is not currently documented. Let's carry on regardless because this method looks especially useful for those situations where a query returns only one row—when using the `COUNT` function to return the number of records in a table, for example. Here's one view of how this method ought to behave: This method returns only one record, and no result set is created. If the second argument is false, the value returned is an array of the first row. If the second argument is true, then only the first column of the first row is returned, and it is returned as a scalar value.

This speculation may make the best sense of how this method ought to work, but it doesn't describe what actually happens. In fact, this method only ever returns the first column and any number of rows. If the second argument is false, then an array is returned; if the second argument is true and only one row is returned, a scalar is returned. On the PHP site, this second argument is identified as `bool first_row_only` and the return type is identified as an `array`. It looks like the return type should be `mixed`. In any case, this method doesn't yet work the way it ought to. We were warned.

There is no requirement that you use the `singleQuery` method instead of `query`. As with MySQL, you can always create a result set and then use the appropriate `fetch` function to retrieve the value of the first row or a specific field. But why return an object or an array when all that's needed is the value of one column? You may use the `singleQuery` method for any kind of query—data manipulation or otherwise—but it was designed specifically for situations where a single value or single column is returned, and is presumably optimized for this situation.

As you can see, there is also an `arrayQuery` method. Like the `singleQuery` method, this method allows us to directly copy results into an array, bypassing the intermediate step of creating a result set. This method is best used when a limited number of records are returned.

MySQL versions prior to 4.1 have no equivalent to the `queryExec` method of SQLite because `queryExec` is specifically designed for use with multiple queries. Multiple, semicolon-separated queries may be passed as a single query string to `queryExec`. (The install script uses this method to create the tables, triggers, and views and to insert records into the `tblresources` table.) This method gives significant performance improvements over repeated querying and performs the same job as the MySQL-improved (the `mysqli` functions added to PHP 5 to support MySQL 4.1) method, `mysqli_multi_query`. If you like, you can of course use this method to execute a single query.

query

Use of this method to create an `SQLiteResult` object is shown in Listing 15-5.

```
$db = new SQLiteDatabasePlus('resources.sqlite');
//alphabet view
$strsql = "SELECT * FROM alphabet";
//use buffered result set to get number of rows
$result = $db->query($strsql);
//create alphabet here
if($result->numRows() > 0){
    echo get_alphabet($result);
}
```

Listing 15-5: query method returns a buffered result set

Remember, an `SQLiteResult` is buffered so you can use the `numRows` method with this result set. It is also iterable, so this result set may be used in a foreach loop. In this, SQLite differs from MySQL. Because `SQLiteResult` implements Iterator, all the iterator methods are present—rewind, next, valid, and current. These methods can be used directly, but their real purpose is to allow an SQLite result set to be used in a foreach loop in exactly the same way that you might use an array. (As you might expect, the rewind method can't be applied to an unbuffered result set.) Only this method and the unbuffered query method return a result set object.

unbufferedQuery

There is no need to buffer the result set returned in Listing 15-6.

```
try{
    $db = new SQLiteDatabasePlus('../dbdir/resources.sqlite');
    $type="Edit";
    //retrieve from db
    $strsql = "SELECT * FROM tblresources ".
        "WHERE id = '$id'";
    //get recordset as row
    $result = $db->unbufferedQuery($strsql);
    $row = $result->fetch();
    //can't use below because returns first column only
    //$row = $db->singleQuery($strsql, false);
    // assume vars same as fields
    while(list($var, $val)=each($row)) {
        $$var=$val;
    }
}catch(SQLiteException $e){
    //debug msg
    echo  $e->getMessage();
  }
}
```

Listing 15-6: The unbufferedQuery method

This listing shows an unbuffered query. In this case, a functional `singleQuery` method would be preferable because we know that only one record will be returned. However, given the problems with `singleQuery`, we use the `unbufferedQuery` method of an `SQLiteDatabase` object to create a result set object and then use the `fetch` method to copy the first row into an array.

arrayQuery

The PHP site warns against using the `arrayQuery` method with queries that return more than 45 records (a somewhat arbitrary number perhaps, but this method stores results in memory so returning a large number of records can exhaust memory). We've used this method in Listing 15-7.

```
$db = new SQLiteDatabasePlus('../dbdir/resources.sqlite');
$db->createFunction('class_id','set_class_id',0);
$sql = "SELECT id, url, email, ".
    "(precedingcopy || ' ' || linktext || ' ' || followingcopy) ".
    "AS copy, linktext, reviewed, class_id() AS classid ".
    "FROM tblresources ".
    "ORDER BY id DESC ".
    "LIMIT $recordoffset,". PERPAGE;
//use arrayQuery
$resultarray = $db->arrayQuery($sql);
...
```

Listing 15-7: Using arrayQuery

As you can see, we know exactly how many records are returned because our SQL has a `LIMIT` clause. Again, this method allows us to bypass creation of a result set.

singleQuery

The code below uses the `singleQuery` method and does exactly what we need—it returns a single scalar value rather than a result set or an array.

```
$totalrecords = $db->singleQuery('Select COUNT(*) FROM
 tblresources', true);
```

queryExec

This method is commonly used to process a transaction. Use the command-line command `.dump` to dump your database or view the file `dump.sql`. You'll see that it is formatted as a transaction. You can recreate an entire database by passing this listing as a string to the `queryExec` method, as we have done with the install script, `db_install_script.php`.

The ability to perform multiple queries using one string does raise security issues. When using this query method, it is especially important to filter data in order to avoid a possible SQL injection attack. For more details, see *php|architect's Guide to PHP Security*.[1]

---

[1] Ilia Alshanetsky, *php|architect's Guide to PHP Security* (Marco Tabini & Associates, Inc., 2005), 73.

Utility Methods

By overriding all the query methods of the SQLiteDatabase class we ensure that any failed query throws an exception. This done, we needn't worry about error trapping whenever we perform a query. The remaining methods of our derived class are utility methods aimed at helping verify data posted from a form. These methods give us an opportunity to explore some of the ways to retrieve metadata from an SQLite database. Find those methods in Listing 15-8.

```
/**
 Get all table names in database
*/
    public function getTableNames(){
        if (!isset($this->tablenames)){
            $this->setTablenames();
        }
        return $this->tablenames;
    }
///////////////////////////////////////////////////////////////
/**
 Retrieve field names/types for specified table
*/
    public function getFields($tablename){
        if (!isset($this->tablenames)){
            $this->setTablenames();
        }
        if (!in_array($tablename, $this->tablenames)){
            throw new SQLiteException("Table $tablename not in database.");
        }
        $fieldnames = array();
        $sql = "PRAGMA table_info('$tablename')";
        $result = $this->unbufferedQuery($sql);
        //no error - bad pragma ignored
        //get name and data type as defined upon creation
        foreach ($result as $row){
            $fieldnames[$row['name']] = $row['type'];
        }
        return $fieldnames;
    }
///////////////////////////////////////////////////////////////
//private methods
/**
    private method - initializes table names array
*/
    private function ❶setTableNames(){
        $sql = "SELECT name ".
            "FROM sqlite_master ".
            "WHERE type = 'table' ".
            "OR type = 'view'";
        $result = $this->unbufferedQuery($sql);
        foreach ($result as $row){
            $this->tablenames[] = $row['name'];
        }
    }
```

Listing 15-8: Metadata methods

The two methods that make use of metadata are setTableNames and getFieldNames. Let's examine ❶ the method setTableNames in Listing 15-8. This method makes use of the table sqlite_master—a table that defines the schema for the database. By querying sqlite_master, we can retrieve the names of all the tables and views in the database. The type field defines the kind of resource, in our case a table or view. This method retrieves the names of all the tables and views and stores them in an array.

Ideally, this method would be called once from the constructor, but the constructor for an SQLite database is declared final, so it may not be overridden.

Pragmas perform a variety of functions in SQLite. One of those functions is to provide information about the database schema—about indices, foreign keys, and tables.

Running the pragma table_info returns a result set that contains the column name and data type. The data type returned is the data type used when the table was created. This may seem pointless—since, excepting one case, all fields are strings—but this information could be used to assist data validation. For example, with access to a data type description, we could programmatically enforce which values are allowed for which fields. Notice that the pragma table_info can also be used with views. However, when used with views, all field types default to numeric.

A word of warning about pragmas: They fail quietly, issuing no warning or error, and there is no guarantee of forward compatibility with newer versions of SQLite.

Getting Metadata

Metadata methods allow us to discover field names at runtime. This is useful when we want to match posted values to the appropriate field in a table. Figure 15-2 shows the form that we will use to post data to the database.

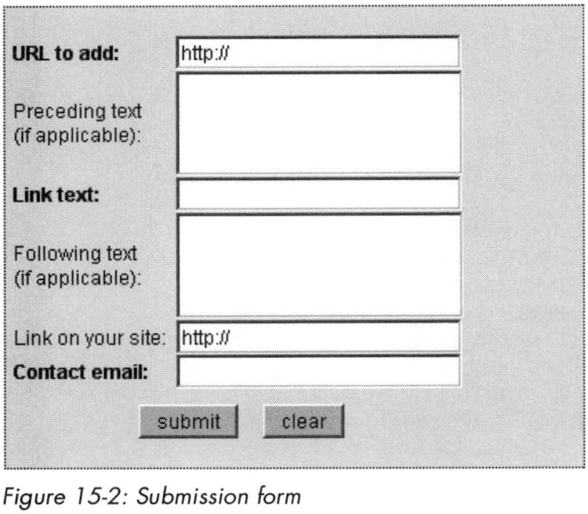

Figure 15-2: Submission form

There's nothing unusual or particularly instructive about this form. However, each control bears the name of its database counterpart. This practice facilitates processing of submitted forms because we can easily match field names with their appropriate values.

Using Metadata

The utility methods that make use of metadata are found in Listing 15-9:

```
/**
 Return clean posted data - check variable names same as field
 names
*/
    public function ❶cleanData($post, $tablename){
        if (!isset($this->tablenames)){
            $this->setTablenames();
        }
        ❷$this->matchNames($post, $tablename);
        //if on remove slashes
        if(get_magic_quotes_gpc()){
            foreach ($post as $key=>$value){
                $post[$key]=stripslashes($value);
            }
        }
        foreach ($post as $key=>$value){
            $post[$key] = htmlentities(sqlite_escape_string($value));
        }
        return $post;
    }
//////////////////////////////////////////////////////////////
/**
  Ensure posted form names match table field names
*/
    public function matchNames($post, $tablename){
        //check is set
        if (!isset($this->tablenames)){
            $this->setTablenames();
        }
        if (count($post) == 0){
            throw new SQLiteException("Array not set.");
        }
        $fields = $this->getFields($tablename);
        foreach ($post as $name=>$value){
            if (!array_key_exists($name, $fields)){
                $message = "No matching column for $name in table
$tablename.";
                throw new SQLiteException($message);
            }
        }
    }
```

Listing 15-9: Utility methods

As you can see in Listing 15-9, ❶ the `cleanData` method verifies that the keys of the posted array match table field names by calling ❷ the `matchNames` method. It throws an exception if they don't. However, it also removes slashes if magic quotes are on. If you regularly use MySQL with magic quotes on, escaping data may be something you never give much thought to. However, unlike MySQL, SQLite does not escape characters by using a backslash; you must use the `sqlite_escape_string` function instead. There is no OO method for doing this.

There is no requirement to call the `cleanData` method, and there may be situations where its use is not appropriate—perhaps where security is a prime concern, so naming form controls with table field names is not advisable. However, it is a convenient way of confirming that the right value is assigned to the right field.

User-Defined Functions

One of the requirements of our application is to highlight recently added links. We are going to achieve this effect by using a different CSS class for links that have been added within the last two weeks. Subtracting the value stored in the `whenadded` field from the current date will determine the links that satisfy this criterion. Were we to attempt this task using MySQL, we could add the following to a SELECT statement:

```
IF(whenadded > SUBDATE(CURDATE(),INTERVAL '14' DAY), 'new',
 'old') AS cssclass
```

This would create a field aliased as `cssclass` that has a value of either `new` or `old`. This field identifies the class of the anchor tag in order to change its appearance using CSS. It's much tidier to perform this operation using SQL rather than by manipulating the `whenadded` field from PHP each time we retrieve a row.

But SQLite has no date subtraction function. In fact, the SQLite site doesn't document any date functions whatsoever. Does this mean that we are stuck retrieving the `whenadded` field from the database and then performing the date operations using PHP? Well, yes and no. SQLite allows for user-defined functions (UDFs). Let's take a look at how this works.

The first thing to do is create a function in PHP to subtract dates—not a terribly difficult task. See the function `check_when_added` in Listing 15-10 for the implementation.

```
function check_when_added($whenadded){
    //less than 2 weeks old
    $type = 'old';
    // use date_default_timezone_set  if available
    $diff = floor(abs(strtotime('now') - strtotime($whenadded))/86400);
    if($diff < 15){
        $type = 'new';
    }
```

```
        return $type;
}
...
    //register function
    $db->❶createFunction('cssclass','check_when_added',1);
    $strsql ="SELECT url, precedingcopy, linktext, followingcopy, ".
        "UPPER(SUBSTR(linktext,1,1)) AS letter, ".
        "cssclass(whenadded) AS type, target ".
        "FROM tblresources ".
        "WHERE reviewed = 1 ".
        "ORDER BY letter ";
    $result = $db->query($strsql);
...
```

Listing 15-10: A user-defined function

Also shown in Listing 15-10 is ❶ the createFunction method of an SQLite-Database, which is used to make check_when_added available from SQLite. Calling this function is as simple as adding the expression cssclass(whenadded) AS type to our SELECT statement. Doing this means that the result set will contain a field called type with either a value of new or no value at all. We can use this value as the class identifier for each resource anchor tag. The new anchors can be highlighted by assigning them different CSS display characteristics.

The back end of our application also makes use of a UDF; improved readability is the motivation behind its creation.

The set_class_id function in Listing 15-11 (❶) shows how the mod operator can be used in a UDF to return alternate values. When this value is used as the id attribute for a tr tag, text can be alternately shaded and unshaded by setting the style characteristics for table rows with the id set to shaded. Again, it is much tidier to return a value in our result set rather than to perform this operation from PHP. Once you are familiar with UDFs you'll see more and more opportunities for using them. Be careful. Using them can become addictive.

```
//add function to SQLite
function ❶set_class_id(){
    static $x = 0;
    $class = 'unshaded';
    if(($x % 2) == 0){
        $class = "shaded";
    }
    $x++;
    return $class;
}
...
$db = new SQLiteDatabasePlus('../dbdir/resources.sqlite');
$db->createFunction('class_id','set_class_id',0);
```

Listing 15-11: UDF shades alternate rows

You can't permanently add a UDF to a database, but the ability to create them certainly compensates for the limited number of functions in SQLite, especially those related to date manipulation. In fact, in my view, this way of subtracting dates is much easier to implement because it doesn't involve looking up or remembering the quirky syntax of functions such as the MySQL SUBDATE function referenced earlier. However, UDFs lack the performance benefits of built-in functions.

Uses and Limitations of SQLite

No database can be all things to all people. SQLite supports any number of simultaneous readers, but a write operation locks the entire database. Version 3 offers some improvement in this respect, but SQLite is still best used in applications with infrequent database updates, like the one described here.

Of course, if access control is important, then SQLite is not the appropriate tool. Because GRANT and REVOKE are not implemented, there can be no database-enforced user restrictions.

However, even a relatively modest application can make use of the advanced capabilities of SQLite. With the application discussed in this chapter, we haven't had to sacrifice anything by using SQLite rather than MySQL. Unavailability of a timestamp field is remedied by use of a trigger. A UDF makes up for SQLite's lack of date manipulation functions. In fact, overall, we achieve better performance because there is no overhead incurred by a database server, and maintenance is reduced through the use of triggers.

Not only has using SQLite simplified our code through the use of views, triggers, and UDFs, as well as by extending the OO interface, but it also makes for cleaner code through its more varied ways of querying a database. In these or similar circumstances, SQLite is definitely a superior choice.

16

USING PDO

Databases are important to any dynamic website. That's why we've had a lot to say about them in this book (too much, some of you may be thinking). However, PHP Data Objects (PDO) can't be ignored because they are packaged with PHP version 5.1 and higher, and they are "something many of the PHP dev team would like to see as the recommended API for database work."[1]

PDO is a data-access abstraction layer that aims for uniform access to any database. That's a pretty good reason for looking at PDO, but what interests us in particular is that the PDO interface is entirely object-oriented (OO). It makes extensive use of the OO improvements to PHP 5. In fact, it cannot be run on lower versions of PHP.

Drivers are available for all the major databases supported by PHP—Oracle, Microsoft SQL Server, PostgreSQL, ODBC, SQLite, and all versions of MySQL up to version 5. So, if you use a variety of different databases, PDO

---

[1] www.zend.com/zend/week/week207.php#Heading6. (Accessed April 14, 2006.)

is especially worth investigating. However, even if you use only one database, PDO can be helpful for switching between versions. Be warned, though, that it is still early days for PDO, and some of the drivers may lack some functionality.

Pros and Cons

The promise of database abstraction is the ability to access any database using identical methods. This gives developers the flexibility to change the back-end database with minimal impact on code. Another advantage of an API such as PDO is a reduced learning curve. Instead of having to learn the specifics of each different database, you can learn one interface and use it with any database. Lastly, with an API you may be able to use features not available to the native database—prepared statements, for example—but more about that later.

On the negative side, a data-access abstraction layer may adversely affect performance and may deprive you of the ability to use non-standard features natively supported by specific databases. It may also introduce an unwanted degree of complexity into your code.

The best way to make a decision about the suitability of PDO is to try it. Converting the SQLite application created in Chapter 15 is a good way to do this. Our SQLite application makes use of a limited number of the features of PDO, so we'll also look at some of PDO's additional capabilities. We won't look at every detail, but this chapter will show you enough to allow you to make an informed decision.

NOTE   *If you are running PHP 5.0.x you can install PDO using PEAR. See the PHP site for instructions. If you install the latest version of PDO you will be able to use SQLite version 3.*

Converting the SQLite Application

The very first thing to realize is that we cannot use our derived class SQLiteDatabasePlus with PDO because the PDO driver for SQLite doesn't know anything about our derived class. We could, of course, extend the PDO class to incorporate the methods we added to our SQLiteDatabasePlus class, but doing so is contrary to the whole purpose of a database abstraction layer. Taking that route would be an implicit admission of defeat right from the start—there wouldn't be one interface for all databases, but instead any number of derived interfaces.

Code Changes

As usual, a complete version of the code discussed in this application is available from the book's website. The directory structure for the files accompanying this chapter is the same as those for Chapter 15, so you shouldn't have trouble finding your way around. Also, as usual, I won't reproduce all the code in this chapter, only relevant sections. We'll start by looking at the constructor.

NOTE *The application we developed in Chapter 15 uses version 2 of SQLite. Take this opportunity to upgrade to SQLite version 3, since PHP 5.1 supports this version. It's appreciably faster than version 2 and handles concurrency better. However, the database format has changed; versions 2 and 3 are incompatible. This is only a minor inconvenience. If you want to get off to a quick start, install the database by running the* db_install _script.php *file found in the* dbdir *directory. This will create an SQLite version 3 database for you. Otherwise, you may download the command-line version of SQLite 3 from the SQLite website, and then see the section "Getting Started" on page 141 for details about using a database dump to install a database. The PDO driver for SQLite version 2 doesn't support the* sqliteCreateFunction *method, so upgrading is required if you want to use this method. Matching the version of the command-line tool with the version of SQLite supported by PHP is equally important in this chapter, because of version incompatibilities. For example, a database created at the command line using SQLite version 3.5.5 will not work properly with the current SQLite PDO driver.*

Constructing a PDO Object

When constructing a PDO database or connection object, a Data Source Name (DSN) is passed as a parameter. A DSN is made up of a driver name, followed by a colon, followed by database-specific syntax. Here's how to create a connection to an SQLite database:

```
$pdo = new PDO('sqlite:resources.sqlite');
```

A PDO object is constructed in the same way as an SQLiteDatabase object except that the driver name must precede the path to the database and be separated from it by a colon.

The createFunction Method

You may recall that one of the deficiencies of SQLite was the lack of built-in functions, especially with respect to date manipulation. We were able to overcome this deficiency by adding functions to SQLite using the createFunction method. Fortunately for us, the developers of PDO have seen fit to incorporate this capability by including the SQLite-specific method sqliteCreateFunction. This saves us some work but also reduces the "abstractness" of the PDO layer—but more about this later.

Exceptions

In Chapter 15 we extended the SQLiteDatabase class in order to throw an exception if a query failed. For that reason we overrode the five existing query methods. The same effect can be achieved with PDO by using only one line of code:

```
$pdo->setAttribute(PDO::ATTR_ERRMODE, PDO::ERRMODE_EXCEPTION);
```

Calling setAttribute against a PDO database connection in this way causes any failed attempt at querying the database to throw a PDOException. This is a very succinct way of dealing with one of the shortcomings of the

SQLite classes. We quickly reap all the benefits of throwing exceptions without having to extend the SQLite database class.

Methods of SQLiteDatabasePlus

Because a PDO connection can be configured to throw exceptions, we don't need the query methods of our derived class SQLiteDatabasePlus. However, the utility methods we added are another matter. The only way to use these methods is to rewrite them as functions. They convert fairly readily, and the metadata queries they employ work as before. The only real difference is that as functions they are not quite as convenient to use. I won't reproduce them here, but they can be found in the dbfunctions.inc file included in this chapter's downloads.

Escaping Input

The cleanData utility method of our derived class incorporated the sqlite_escape_string function to escape input before insertion into the database. The equivalent PDO method is quote. Be aware that this method not only escapes single quotation marks, but also encloses the item quoted within quotation marks. If you need to manipulate data prior to inserting it, quote should only be called immediately prior to insertion. For portability reasons, the PHP site recommends using prepare rather than quote. We'll investigate this method more fully when we discuss statements, in the section "Additional Capabilities of PDO" on page 161.

Query Methods

One of the attractions of SQLite is its variety of query methods. If you need a quick refresher, see the section "Query Methods" on page 148. In this section we're going to compare SQLite's query methods to what's available using PDO.

The difference between the object models of SQLite and PDO makes a direct comparison a bit awkward. Principally, querying a PDO connection returns a statement object, and this statement effectively becomes a result set once it is executed. As already mentioned, we'll cover statements in the section "Additional Capabilities of PDO" on page 161, but for the moment we can treat them as identical to result sets.

The five query methods of SQLite are singleQuery, execQuery, arrayQuery, query, and unbufferedQuery. We'll discuss each SQLite query method in turn.

The singleQuery method returns a single column as an array, bypassing the need to create a result set. To mimic it we would use a PDO query to return a statement and then call fetchColumn against this statement. The fetchColumn method can return any column in the current row.

The execQuery method of an SQLite result set can execute multiple, semicolon-separated queries. PDO can easily mimic this behavior—in fact this is something that statements excel at.

As you might expect, returning an array in the fashion of arrayQuery is also easily handled by PDO by calling the fetchAll method against a statement.

The two remaining query methods of SQLite, query and unbufferedQuery, return SQLiteResult and SQLiteUnbuffered objects, respectively. PDO statements are comparable to unbuffered result sets rather than buffered ones, so the unbuffered behavior is easily reproduced. Our SQLite application uses buffered result sets in cases where we need to know that there are records returned or where the specific number of records is required. To buffer records using PDO you can use the fetchAll method of a statement to return an array. A record count can be obtained by using the count function on the returned array. Alternately, calling the function empty on the statement returned by a query will determine whether there is at least one record.

In general, when querying the database, it looks like some efficiencies have been lost. What is a single process using SQLite becomes a two-step process with PDO. Using two methods instead of one can make code more complicated. However, as we'll soon see, there are some important advantages to the PDO methods, and in some cases this two-step process can be simplified.

Additional Capabilities of PDO

Converting one application certainly doesn't tell the whole story about PDO, so let's have a look at some of the other capabilities of PDO. There are three PDO classes: PDO; the database or connection class, PDOStatement; and PDORow. By far the most interesting and unfamiliar class is the statement class, and this is where we'll concentrate our attention. We'll briefly discuss PDORow when we come to the fetchObject method of the statement class.

The PDO Class

So far in this book we've created our own connection class and used the SQLiteDatabase class—classes that have many similarities to PDO. With this experience, I needn't say a lot about the PDO class.

I've already mentioned the quote, setAttribute, and query methods of the PDO class. For databases such as SQLite that support transactions, this class also has methods to begin, commit, or roll back transactions.

The most important method, however, is prepare. This method is similar to the query method in that it also returns a PDOStatement. The major difference is that query is typically used for SQL statements that are issued once and prepare for queries that will be issued a number of times.

PDOStatement

In the conversion of our application from SQLite to PDO, in some cases the difference between a result set and a statement isn't apparent at all. For example, the snippet of SQLite code to display all the resources in our database (from the file getresources.php) is shown in Listing 16-1.

```
$result = $db->query($strsql);
if(!empty($result)){
    $previous = "";
    foreach ($result as $row){
        foreach ($row as $key => $value){
            ...
```

Listing 16-1: Displaying resources

The equivalent PDO code is identical. In one case, the variable $db represents an SQLiteDatabasePlus, and in the other it represents a PDO. Likewise the $result variable is an SQLiteResult or a PDOStatement. Because result sets and statements are both iterable, they can be used in the same way within foreach loops. In this case, using PDO takes no more steps than using SQLite directly.

This similarity between a result set and a statement makes it easy to start using statements, but it also masks important differences. These differences are more apparent when the prepare method is used.

prepare

Instead of using the query method to create a PDOStatement object, the code $result = $db->query($strsql); in Listing 16-1 can be changed to the following:

```
$result = $db->prepare($strsql);
$result->execute();
```

I have already hinted at one of the advantages of using prepare instead of query. Any variables used in the parameter to the prepare method will automatically be quoted. This is an easier and more portable way of escaping quotes than using the quote method. If used exclusively, you needn't worry about forgetting to quote an SQL statement. This is a security advantage that will protect against SQL injection attacks.

This is one way in which a statement is superior to a result set, but it is not the most important difference. Statements are more commonly used to insert multiple records into a database, and they do this more efficiently than a series of individual SQL statements. This is what is referred to as a *prepared statement.*

Prepared Statements

There are a number of ways that statements can be used with both input and output parameters. We'll content ourselves with one example of a prepared statement used to make multiple inserts. The SQLite application in Chapter 15 has no need for multiple inserts, so we'll create a simple new example.

Suppose you have an ecommerce application. The inventory numbers for various purchased items are stored in an array. Here's how we can update our database using a prepared statement:

```
//$pdo is an instance of a PDO connection
$orderid = "200";
$array_skus = array(1345, 2899, 6502);
$strsql = "INSERT INTO tblorderitems (orderid, inventorynumber) ".
    " Values ($orderid, ❶? ) ";
$stmt = $pdo->prepare($strsql);
$stmt->❷bindParam(1, $number);
foreach ($array_skus as $number){
  $stmt->❸execute();
}
```

This is a fairly simple example of a prepared statement, but it will give you an understanding of how statements work. A replaceable parameter (❶) is indicated by a question mark, this parameter ❷ is bound to the variable $number, and each iteration of the foreach loop ❸ executes the query, inserting a different value.

Using statements is much more efficient than separately querying the database. The performance improvements are due to the fact that after a parameterized query is first executed, for each subsequent query, only the bound data needs to be passed.

Remember, there's no such thing as a prepared statement in SQLite. The developers of PDO thought it important to support this feature for all databases regardless of native support. Using PDO is a good way to familiarize yourself with statements and makes it easy to switch to a database that supports this capability.

Fetching Objects

For an OO programmer, the ability to retrieve rows as objects is important. PDO has a number of ways of doing this. An easy way of doing this is to create an instance of the PDORow class in the following way:

```
$stmt = $pdo->query( "SELECT * FROM tblresources", PDO::FETCH_LAZY );
$pdorow = $stmt->fetch();
```

There is also a fetchObject method that can be used to create an instance of a specific class. Supposing we have defined a class called RowInfo, creating an instance of that class is done in this way:

```
$row = $stmt->fetchObject('RowInfo');
```

This method is perhaps the simplest way to create an object. You can use it with an existing class or, if you don't specify a class, it will create an instance of stdClass, the generic object class.

What these various ways of creating objects have in common is that they instantiate an object, creating data members from the columns of the current row.

PDOStatement also has a method, getColumnMeta, to dynamically retrieve metadata about the current query. By using this method in conjunction with one of the create object methods and adding a magic get method to the class you're instantiating, it is easy to retrieve the data members of any object created from any query without knowing the structure of that query beforehand.[2] Perhaps our criticisms of magic set and get methods in Chapter 13 were a little harsh.

NOTE *SQLite has a procedural version of fetchObject that returns a stdClass object. It is documented as a result set method but not yet implemented.*

---

[2] You could, of course, query the sqlite_master table for this information, but the PDO method provides a database-independent way of doing this.

Assessment

We've touched on a number of the capabilities of PDO. We've used some of them in our application, but not all of them. This is by no means a definitive overview of PDO, but we certainly have enough information to make a judgment about the utility of this data-access abstraction layer.

Our application behaves exactly as it did without PDO. We haven't had to sacrifice any functionality and some things were much easier to implement—catching exceptions, for example. All our queries, triggers, and views work in exactly the same way. One minor inconvenience was converting the utility methods of our derived class, but we were able to implement them procedurally without loss of functionality. The object model of PDO is perhaps a little more difficult, but along with this we've gained the ability to use prepared statements should we need them. No question—PDO works well with SQLite.

But what if we decided to use a MySQL back-end instead? How many changes would we have to make? Beyond changing the driver, the most obvious change would be removal of the SQLite-specific function `sqliteCreateFunction`. As noted in Chapter 15, this could be replaced by the MySQL function `SUBDATE`. Likewise, any other operators or functions not used by MySQL would have to be changed.

Another option would be to use standard SQL wherever possible. The date manipulation functions could be ignored, and this task performed from within PHP. That's a choice each developer will have to make for themselves, but I expect most won't quickly give up on hard-won knowledge about specific SQL dialects.

Is It the Holy Grail?

One very legitimate concern might be voiced over the inclusion of the SQLite-specific method `sqliteCreateFunction`, and this is certainly not the only database-specific capability provided by PDO.[3] Doesn't providing database-specific functionality do exactly what we refrained from doing at the start—namely, extending the PDO class?

The short answer is, unquestionably, yes. But the whole notion of a perfect database abstraction layer is a Holy Grail—glimpsed here and there but never grasped. Providing some database-specific functionality is a sensible compromise and an impetus to use PDO. As always with PHP, utility and not purity of concept is paramount. The important thing to note is that each developer can make their own decision about an acceptable level of database abstraction by incorporating database-specific methods and database-specific SQL or not as the case may be. However, in one respect there's no choice at all: If you choose to use PDO, you must take an OO approach.

---

[3] The constant `PDO::MYSQL_ATTR_USE_BUFFERED_QUERY` can be used to create a buffered result set with a MySQL database. Using `fetchAll` is the more abstract or database-neutral approach.

SETTING UP PHP 5

All recent major Linux distributions (SUSE, Fedora, Mandriva, and Debian among them) come with support for PHP 5. If your distribution doesn't support version 5, the easiest solution is to locate and install an updated Red Hat Package Manager (RPM). Otherwise, you will need to download the PHP source code and configure and install PHP yourself. (If you want to install PHP as a static module, you will also have to download the source code for Apache.) Instructions for compiling PHP are readily available at http://php.net, but taking this route requires familiarity with working from the command line in Linux.

PHP 5 also runs under Windows using Internet Information Server (IIS) or Apache Web Server. Although Windows does not come with built-in support for PHP, installing PHP is a relatively easy task. The Windows PHP installer will get you up and running in minutes, but it is not meant for a production server—it's better to perform a manual installation. Comprehensive instructions for doing this are provided at http://php.net/install, but here's a brief overview of the process.

Download the Windows binary from the PHP website, and install it to a directory on your hard drive. If you are using IIS, find the web server configuration window and map the `.php` file extension to the location of the php program.

For Apache Web Server 2, you will need to make the following changes to the `httpd.conf` file:

```
LoadModule php5_module "c:/php-5.1/php5apache2.dll"
```

If you are running version 1.3 of Apache, use the `php5apache.dll` file.

You will also have to add an application type to your configuration file. The example below will process files with the extensions `.php` or `.inc` as PHP files.

```
AddType application/x-httpd-php .php .inc
```

Comprehensive instructions for installing and configuring Apache under Windows can be found at http://httpd.apache.org/docs/2.0/platform/windows.html, but, again, the process is fairly straightforward.

The code contained in this book should run equally well regardless of which combination of operating system and web server you choose.

php.ini Settings

The `php.ini` file controls configuration settings for PHP and is typically found in the `c:\windows` directory on Windows systems and in the `/etc` directory on Linux systems. When installing PHP 5 it is best to use the example `php.ini` file with the default settings. This section deals with changes that affect OOP. (For an overview of all the changes, see http://php.net/install.)

There is only one new configuration setting that relates directly to changes made to the object model in PHP 5. Specifically, showing the default setting, this is:

```
zend.ze1_compatibility_mode = Off
```

If you change this setting to On, objects will be copied by value in the manner of PHP 4. (See the section "__clone" on page 116 for more details about how objects are copied.) This option is provided in order to facilitate migration from PHP 4 to PHP 5. It should be used for this purpose only, as it is unlikely to be supported in any upcoming versions of PHP.

Another setting that has some bearing on changes made to the object model in PHP 5 is

```
allow_call_time_pass_reference = Off
```

This setting controls whether a warning is issued when a variable is passed by reference when making a function call. With this setting off, calling a function in the following way will issue a warning and will not pass $some_variable by reference:

```
some_function(&$some_variable);
```

The recommended way of passing a variable by reference is by declaring the parameter as a reference in the function definition, like so:

```
function some_function ( &$some_variable ) {
    ...
}
```

If you do this, then there is no need to use an ampersand when passing a variable to some_function. (If you are upgrading PHP 4 code that passes objects at call time by reference, you can remove ampersands entirely. You will recall that in PHP 5 objects are automatically passed by reference, so there is no need for an ampersand at call time *or* in the function definition.) It is a good idea to upgrade your code to pass by reference in the recommended manner because call-time pass by reference is unlikely to be supported in future versions of PHP.

E_STRICT

A new error level, E_STRICT, has been introduced and is especially useful in the context of OOP. If you set error reporting to this value, a warning will be issued when deprecated functions or coding styles are used. Error level E_ALL does not encompass E_STRICT, so include this error level explicitly in the php.ini file in the following way:

```
error_reporting = E_ALL|E_STRICT
```

To see how this setting can be useful, suppose, in the style of PHP 4, that you do the following:

```
$obj1 =& new Person();
```

With error reporting set to E_STRICT and display_errors set to on, you'll receive the message:

```
Strict Standards: Assigning the return value of new by reference is
deprecated...
```

Other actions also raise a warning when error reporting is set to E_STRICT:

- Use of is_a instead of instanceof.
- Invoking a non-static function statically (this error is soon to be E_FATAL). However, calling a static method against an instance variable does not raise a warning.
- Use of var instead of public, private, or protected (prior to version 5.1.3).
- Changing the number of parameters or the type hint when overriding a method in a derived class.

Making sure that your code follows strict standards can help ensure that it is forward compatible especially with respect to calling dynamic methods statically.

Don't Escape Twice

There's a final setting that has some bearing on OOP.

It's worthwhile noting that the default setting for magic quotes is

```
magic_quotes_gpc = Off
```

As you have seen, methods such as the prepare method of the PDO class automatically escape database queries. So, if magic quotes are turned on, you can easily corrupt data by escaping it twice. Use care if you change this setting.

B

CONVERSION TABLE: PHP 4 AND PHP 5

PHP 5	PHP 4	Notes
Access Modifiers		
public	var	All instance variables and methods are public under PHP 4. In PHP 4 var is used for data members only; methods have no access modifiers.
private	var	
protected	var	
Prefixes		
parent::	parent::	
ClassName::	ClassName::	Used for referencing constants or static data members or methods from inside the class or externally (substituting ClassName as appropriate).
self::	N/A	Used as ClassName:: but only internally.

(continued)

PHP 5	PHP 4	Notes
Other Keywords		
abstract	N/A	Use empty methods for a reasonable imitation.
class	class	
extends	extends	
interface	N/A	
implements	N/A	
final	N/A	
static	N/A	In PHP 4 you can mimic static methods using the class name and the scope resolution operator.
const	N/A	
try and catch	N/A	There is no Exception class in PHP 4, so there are no try blocks.
function	function	Methods are defined using the function keyword.
Magic Methods		
__construct	class name	In PHP 5 you may still use the class name, but for reasons of forward compatibility it is better to use the magic method.
__destruct	N/A	In PHP 4 you can use register_shutdown_function() to mimic a destructor.
__toString	N/A	In PHP 4 you can create a function to do the equivalent, but it will not be invoked magically by print or echo.
__sleep and __wakeup	__sleep and __wakeup	
__set, __get and __call	N/A	
__isset and __unset	N/A	
__clone	N/A	
__autoload	N/A	

(continued)

PHP 5	PHP 4	Notes
Operators		
function foo($variable)	function foo(&$variable)	Note that this example shows a function declaration, not a function call. Passing objects by reference explicitly is recommended in PHP 4, but not required in PHP 5 because objects are automatically passed by reference. In PHP 5, you only ever need use a reference as a parameter with non-objects.
foo(&$var);	Deprecated.	Call-time pass by reference is deprecated in PHP 5. For more information see Appendix A. Use a reference in the function definition when passing non-objects (not required for objects, as noted above).
=	=&	In PHP 5 assignment of objects is equivalent to assignment by reference under PHP 4.
$obj = new ClassName();	$obj =& new ClassName();	In PHP 5 new automatically returns a reference. PHP 4 style is deprecated.
clone	=	In PHP 4 assignment clones an object.
instanceof	is_a	is_a is the only function of the Class/Object functions that has been deprecated (as of PHP 5).
Other Changes of Interest		
get_class, get_class_methods, and get_parent_class	get_class, get_class_methods, and get_parent_class	In PHP 5 these methods return a case-sensitive result.
functionName(ObjectType $o)	N/A	In PHP 5 you may type hint object parameters to functions. As of PHP 5.1 you may also type hint arrays. Type hinting return values of functions or methods is also planned. This will, of course, only apply to objects.

GLOSSARY

A

abstract method   A method that is declared but not defined. Any class that contains an abstract method must use this keyword in the class definition. All of the methods of an interface are abstract. A class that has only abstract methods is a pure abstract class.

accessor method   A public method used to retrieve or change data members. Accessor methods are also called get and set methods. (It is considered good programming practice to make data members private and alter or retrieve them only through accessor methods.)

aggregate class   A class having at least one data member that is itself an object

application programming interface (API)   The public face of a class

Asynchronous JavaScript and XML (AJAX)   A web development technique that incorporates JavaScript, XML, and other tools; typically entails use of the JavaScript DOM object XMLHttpElement to communicate with the server and refresh web page elements without reloading the entire page

B

backward compatibility   A characteristic of a version of a programming language or application that allows it to work with previous versions or files created using previous versions

base class   A class from which other classes are derived; also called a *parent class* or superclass

C

call time   The time at which a function or method is invoked

Cascading Style Sheets (CSS)   A web design technique that separates the content and presentation of a web page. Style sheets are cascading because they can be applied from an external file, within the style section of a web page, or inline, and each lower level overrides any style characteristics defined previously.

child class   See *derived class.*

class   A complex data type that typically includes both data members and methods; the most fundamental element of OOP

class variable   A static data member belonging to the class as a whole and not to any specific instance

client programmer   The user of a class rather than the creator or originator of a class; sometimes referred to as a user programmer

const   A keyword, new to PHP 5, used to define constant class data

constructor   A special function called when objects are created. In PHP 4 the constructor uses the class name. This style of constructor still works in PHP 5, but the recommended practice is to define the method __construct.

D

data hiding   The ability to restrict and control access to data members; also called data protection

data member   A variable declared within a class but outside any method; also called a *property* or *instance* variable

Data Source Name (DSN)   The specification of the driver and resources necessary to create a PHP Data Object

deprecated   No longer recommended usage, obsolete; for example, "The is_a function is deprecated as of PHP 5." (The deprecated entity will eventually be extinct from the language.)

design pattern   A general description of a solution to a design problem; somewhat akin to an abstract class or interface, but even less specific

destructor   The opposite of a constructor, invoked automatically whenever an object goes out of scope; usually ensures that any resources, such as file handles, are properly disposed of

derived class   Any class that has a *base* or *parent class*; also called a *child class* or subclass

Document Object Model (DOM)   The representation of an HTML or XML document in object-oriented fashion

E

encapsulation   A process that allows implementation details irrelevant to a client programmer to be kept private and not exposed as public methods or public data members; related to data hiding but more comprehensive

extends   The keyword used when inheriting from a class; for example, class `Canary extends Bird`

Extensible HyperText Markup Language (XHTML)   See *XHTML.*

Extensible Markup Language (XML)   See *XML.*

F

final   A modifier applied to methods or classes that restricts inheritance; a `final` class cannot be extended, and a `final` method cannot be overridden

forward compatibility   Writing code with future upgrades to the language in mind; for example, avoiding the use of deprecated coding styles

G

garbage collection   Automatic memory management that removes references to resources that are no longer used

H

HTML (HyperText Markup Language)   A simple markup language derived from SGML and used to create web pages

I

implements   The keyword that replaces extends when inheriting an interface rather than a class

inheritance   The ability of an OO language to pass the methods and data members of an existing class on to a new class

instance   A specific occurrence of a class; creation of a class object is referred to as instantiation

interface   1. A keyword in PHP indicating a class that declares methods but does not define them. PHP allows multiple interfaces to be inherited. 2. The public methods of a class.

Iterator   An interface, built in to PHP 5, that allows objects to be traversed

J

Javadoc format   A format for internal comments; the getDocComment method of the reflection classes can extract comments formatted in this way

M

magic method   A method that begins with a double underscore and is usually invoked indirectly. __sleep and __wakeup are magic methods in PHP 4. A number of magic methods are new to PHP 5, most importantly the __construct and __clone methods.

metadata   Data that describes other data; for example, information about the structure of a database

method   A function defined within the scope of a class

Multipurpose Internet Mail Extensions (MIME)   The standard Internet email format, but more broadly, a content type specification such as "image/jpeg"

N

name/value pair   The format for a query string passed to a web page; any query string is composed of one or more name/value pairs. Access is provided by the global arrays $_POST or $_GET, with the name functioning as the array key.

overloaded   A characteristic of a method; describes the ability to behave differently when supplied with different parameters. In PHP, this term is usually applied to the __call, __set, and __get methods, in the sense that one method may handle a number of different methods or properties. (Because PHP is a weakly-typed language, you cannot have an overloaded method as understood in some other OO languages—namely, one method name but different method signatures.)

override   The act of redefining the method of a parent class in a child class

P

parent class   See *base class*.

PHP Data Object (PDO)   A group of classes that provides a data-access abstraction layer, included by default with PHP version 5.1 and higher; drivers are available for databases commonly used with PHP

PHP Extension and Application Repository (PEAR)   A library of open-source code, organized into packages that are easily installed using the PEAR installer

polymorphism   Properly speaking, the ability to copy a child object into a variable of the parent type and still invoke the methods of the child against that parent object; used somewhat loosely when applied to PHP

private   A keyword used to modify the methods or data members of a class; private elements can only be accessed from within the class or indirectly through accessor methods and cannot be inherited

procedural   A type of computer language that makes extensive use of procedures or function calls; for example, the C language is a procedural language, while PHP can be used procedurally or in an object-oriented fashion

property   Synonymous with *instance* variable or *data member*

protected   A keyword that can be applied to methods or data members. Like the private elements of a class, protected elements may not be accessed outside the class; unlike private elements, protected elements are inherited by derived classes.

prototype   The declaration of a function prior to defining it (some languages, but not PHP, require this); can be applied to the declaration of a method, especially with regard to interfaces

public   A keyword that modifies the methods or data members of a class; public methods of a class, sometimes referred to as a class's *interface,* can be invoked against an instance of the class, and are inherited by derived classes

Q

query string   One or more name/value pairs passed to a web page as part of the URL

R

RSS (Really Simple Syndication or Rich Site Summary)   Often referred to as a news feed; conforms to a specific XML format

S

scope   The context within which a variable can be accessed. A variable defined within a method may be referenced only within that method, whereas the scope of an instance variable is the entire class.

scope resolution operator   The operator ::, used in conjunction with the class name when referencing constants or static methods

shallow copy   A copy of an object that is not independent of the original. When copying aggregate objects, special care must be taken to avoid creating a shallow copy.

signature   A unique property of a function or method, consisting of the function or method name and the number and data type of its parameters;

used loosely when applied to PHP. In strongly-typed languages, methods can have the same name as long as the number or type of parameters differ and they have unique signatures.

Standard Generalized Markup Language (SGML)   An international standard for representing documents; both HTML and XML are derived from SGML

Standard PHP Library (SPL)   A collection of classes built in to PHP

static   A modifier applied to a class method or variable that allows access to that element without having to create an instance of the class; static variables or methods are common to all instances of a class

studly caps   A naming convention in which each appended word of a compound name is capitalized; sometimes referred to as CamelCase. Class names use upper CamelCase (as in `DirectoryItem`) and methods use lower CamelCase (as in `getName`).

T

type hinting   The ability to restrict the kind of object passed to a function or method by preceding a parameter name with an object type in the function or method definition; arrays may also be type hinted as of PHP 5.1

W

weakly-typed   Used to describe a language, like PHP, in which data type identification is not required when declaring a variable

Web Services Definition Language (WSDL)   An XML format that describes a web service

World Wide Web Consortium (W3C)   The organization responsible for developing standards for the World Wide Web

wrapper method   A method that simply encloses an existing function call

X

XHTML (eXtensible HyperText Markup Language)   An XML-compliant form of HTML

XML (eXtensible Markup Language)   A markup language, like HTML, derived from SGML; XML-compliant documents must meet stricter requirements than HTML documents

Z

Zend engine   The scripting engine that underlies PHP; it was entirely rewritten for PHP 5 in order to support the improved OO capabilities

INDEX

W

W3C (World Wide Web
    Consortium), 100
__wakeup, magic method, 116, 170
warnings, for deprecated functions,
    14, 15
web developers, 1, 3, 4
web hosting, 16
Web Service Definition Language
    (WSDL). *See* WSDL
web services, 13, 104, 105, 110
well-formed XML document, 102
World Wide Web Consortium
    (W3C). *See* W3C

wrapper method, 20–21, 67, 70, 115
WSDL (Web Services Definition
    Language), 104, 105, 106

X

XHTML, 100
XML (eXtensible Markup
    Language), 13, 99–101
XML toolkit, 13, 100

Z

Zend engine, 15
zend.ze1_compatibility_mode, 166

Electronic Frontier Foundation
Defending Freedom in the Digital World

Free Speech. Privacy. Innovation. Fair Use. Reverse Engineering. **If you care about these rights in the digital world, then you should join the Electronic Frontier Foundation (EFF). EFF was founded in 1990 to protect the rights of users and developers of technology. EFF is the first to identify threats to basic rights online and to advocate on behalf of free expression in the digital age.**

> ## The Electronic Frontier Foundation Defends Your Rights!
> ## Become a Member Today!
> ## http://www.eff.org/support/

Current EFF projects include:

Protecting your fundamental right to vote. Widely publicized security flaws in computerized voting machines show that, though filled with potential, this technology is far from perfect. EFF is defending the open discussion of e-voting problems and is coordinating a national litigation strategy addressing issues arising from use of poorly developed and tested computerized voting machines.

Ensuring that you are not traceable through your things. Libraries, schools, the government and private sector businesses are adopting radio frequency identification tags, or RFIDs – a technology capable of pinpointing the physical location of whatever item the tags are embedded in. While this may seem like a convenient way to track items, it's also a convenient way to do something less benign: track people and their activities through their belongings. EFF is working to ensure that embrace of this technology does not erode your right to privacy.

Stopping the FBI from creating surveillance backdoors on the Internet. EFF is part of a coalition opposing the FBI's expansion of the Communications Assistance for Law Enforcement Act (CALEA), which would require that the wiretap capabilities built into the phone system be extended to the Internet, forcing ISPs to build backdoors for law enforcement.

Providing you with a means by which you can contact key decision-makers on cyber-liberties issues. EFF maintains an action center that provides alerts on technology, civil liberties issues and pending legislation to more than 50,000 subscribers. EFF also generates a weekly online newsletter, EFFector, and a blog that provides up-to-the minute information and commentary.

Defending your right to listen to and copy digital music and movies. The entertainment industry has been overzealous in trying to protect its copyrights, often decimating fair use rights in the process. EFF is standing up to the movie and music industries on several fronts.

Check out all of the things we're working on at http://www.eff.org and join today or make a donation to support the fight to defend freedom online.

ELECTRONIC FRONTIER FOUNDATION · 454 SHOTWELL STREET · SAN FRANCISCO, CA 94110 · 415.436.9333

THE BOOK OF PYTHON
From the Tip of the Tongue to the End of the Tale

by JOHN A. GOEBEL, ADIL HASAN, *and* FRANCESCO SAFAI TEHRANI

The Book of Python is a complete reference to the Python programming language. It begins with a discussion of Python's programming environment, then moves on to more advanced topics, including object-oriented programming, interacting with operating systems, creating GUIs and database interfaces, network programming, XML, web programming, and much more. To aid programmers in their day-to-day use of this book, functions and modules are cross-referenced throughout and multiple examples illustrate how to use Python.

SEPTEMBER 2006, 1000 PP., $49.95 ($64.95 CDN)
ISBN 1-59327-103-4

HOW LINUX WORKS
What Every Superuser Should Know

by BRIAN WARD

How Linux Works shows how the Linux system functions so that system administrators can devise their own solutions to problems. Readers will find coverage of devices, disks, filesystems, and the kernel, how Linux boots, essential system files, servers, and utilities, network configuration and services, shell scripts, development tools, compiling software from source code, maintaining the kernel, configuring and manipulating peripherals, printing, backups, sharing files with Samba, network file transfer, buying hardware for Linux, and user environments.

MAY 2004, 368 PP., $37.95 ($55.95 CDN)
ISBN 1-59327-035-6

WEBBOTS, SPIDERS, AND SCREEN SCRAPERS

by MICHAEL SCHRENK

The Internet is bigger and better than what a mere browser allows. *Webbots, Spiders, and Screen Scrapers* is for developers and business managers looking to unlock the competitive advantages of nontraditional online approaches. Readers will learn how to write stealthy webbots that read email, emulate online forms, auto-authenticate, manage cookies, and handle encryption. Sample projects reinforce these new skills so that readers can create more sophisticated webbots and spiders to track online prices, create anonymous browsing environments, bid on auctions in their closing moments, and more.

SEPTEMBER 2006, 352 PP., $39.95 ($51.95 CDN)
ISBN 1-59327-120-4

THE BOOK OF JAVASCRIPT, 2ND EDITION
A Practical Guide to Interactive Web Pages

by THAU!

The Book of JavaScript teaches readers how to add interactivity, animation, and other tricks to their websites with JavaScript. Rather than provide a series of cut-and-paste scripts, thau! takes the reader through a series of real world JavaScript code examples with an emphasis on understanding. Each chapter focuses on a few important JavaScript features, shows how professional websites incorporate them, and shows readers how they might add those features to their own websites. This thoroughly updated 2nd edition includes coverage of Ajax, revised appendices, and new examples throughout. Summary sections and assignments close each chapter, making the book perfect for use in college courses or independent study. The accompanying CD includes code and images for every example, answers to assignments, script libraries for hard-to-program applications, and many useful software programs.

JULY 2006, 456 PP. W/CD, $39.95 ($51.95 CDN)
ISBN 1-59327-106-9

WICKED COOL PHP

by WILLIAM STEINMETZ

Rather than explain the basics of PHP, *Wicked Cool PHP* provides scripts that can be implemented immediately to make programmers' lives easier. It includes scripts not found in any other books, including scripts for processing credit cards, getting live shipping quotes, and accepting PayPal payments online. Author William Steinmetz approaches the limitations of PHP frankly and honestly, showing readers where security holes might be created by novice programmers and suggesting workarounds for when PHP fails. Readers will learn how to create robot-blocking security images and on-the-fly graphs to embed in web pages, access email accounts with PHP, design screen scrapers to connect to other sites and download information from them, and much more.

JULY 2006, 304 PP., $29.95 ($38.95 CDN)
ISBN 1-59327-102-6

PHONE:
800.420.7240 OR
415.863.9900
MONDAY THROUGH FRIDAY,
9 A.M. TO 5 P.M. (PST)

FAX:
415.863.9950
24 HOURS A DAY,
7 DAYS A WEEK

EMAIL:
SALES@NOSTARCH.COM

WEB:
WWW.NOSTARCH.COM

MAIL:
NO STARCH PRESS
555 DE HARO ST, SUITE 250
SAN FRANCISCO, CA 94107
USA

COLOPHON

Object-Oriented PHP was laid out in Adobe FrameMaker. The font families used are New Baskerville for body text, Futura for headings and tables, and Dogma for titles.

The book was printed and bound at Malloy Incorporated in Ann Arbor, Michigan. The paper is Glatfelter Thor 60# Antique, which is made from 50 percent recycled materials, including 30 percent postconsumer content. The book uses a RepKover binding, which allows it to lay flat when open.

UPDATES

Visit **www.nostarch.com/oophp.htm** for updates and other information. Errata, additional resources, and all code samples included in the book are available at **http://objectorientedphp.com**.